One Spanish Summer

And Other Stories from the Road

A Professional Woman's
Search for Adventure

Juliette Robertson

BALBOA
PRESS

A DIVISION OF HAY HOUSE

Balboa Press books may be ordered through booksellers or by contacting:

Balboa Press
A Division of Hay House
1663 Liberty Drive
Bloomington, IN 47403
www.balboapress.com
1 (877) 407-4847

Because of the dynamic nature of the Internet, any web addresses or links contained in this book may have changed since publication and may no longer be valid. The views expressed in this work are solely those of the author and do not necessarily reflect the views of the publisher, and the publisher hereby disclaims any responsibility for them.

The author of this book does not dispense medical advice or prescribe the use of any technique as a form of treatment for physical, emotional, or medical problems without the advice of a physician, either directly or indirectly. The intent of the author is only to offer information of a general nature to help you in your quest for emotional and spiritual well-being. In the event you use any of the information in this book for yourself, which is your constitutional right, the author and the publisher assume no responsibility for your actions.

Any people depicted in stock imagery provided by Thinkstock are models, and such images are being used for illustrative purposes only. Certain stock imagery © Thinkstock.

Print information available on the last page.

ISBN: 978-1-5043-0543-3 (sc)
ISBN: 978-1-5043-0544-0 (e)

Balboa Press rev. date: 09/27/2017

Dedication

For my children, Jordon and Lauren

I hope you never fear those mountains in the distance. Never settle for the path of least resistance. Living might mean taking chances but they're worth taking. Loving might be a mistake but it's worth making. Don't let some bleeding heart, leave you bitter. When you come close to selling out, reconsider. Give the heavens above more than just a passing glance, and when you get the choice to sit it out or dance, I hope you dance.

Lee Ann Womack: American Singer/songwriter: *"I Hope Your Dance"*

Mum xx

With Thanks

To the wonderful older and wiser women who have walked with me through various chapters of my life, and kept me buoyant with their humour, courage, unfailing love and belief in me: My gorgeous mum, Angie Robertson, and my business and life mentors, Carol Stewart, Elana Lantry, Patricia Snider and Ingrid Kent.

Contents

Other Stories from the Road

Foreword

What an amazing book about the human spirit. I believe as a society we have moved away from the essence of living. We are too often focused on the next reality TV show or how many 'likes' we can hand out for the day. We seem more interested in living our life voyeuristically through others than confronting our own.

'One Spanish Summer; and Other Stories from the Road' is a book about truly living. It is a refreshing journey - seen through the eyes of someone who has really embraced life. It's a book about courage and adventure. The world opens for those few brave souls who confront life and have the courage to face their fears.

Real growth in life only comes from extending beyond your limits. The greater the fear, the greater the growth. It is who we have to become to overcome our fear that is most relevant in life. The reward for those who meet this challenge is an inner peace, confidence and level of self-awareness not experienced by many. There is a freedom that comes from living your life consistent with your purpose, without fear of what others may think of you.

This book will both inspire you and challenge you to ask better quality questions of yourself. There is something very magical about the human spirit when ignited with passion. Enjoy Juliette's journey and then grab your own with both hands.

Stephen Bock
Australian Summiteer of Mt. Everest,
Aerobatic pilot and motivational speaker.

Preface

Hot sweat, tanned bodies. His happiness had poured over me all day, quenching my thirst for his deep kisses and laughter, two lovers romping like puppies along the beach for hours, playing in the dunes. And now as evening fell, he toyed with me still, pulling me closer suggestively, teasing me with the promise of endless days together. Then with a soft farewell caress, he bowed, splashed gold across the darkening sky, smiled lovingly and disappeared below the horizon. He was gone. I watched him go, his light still dancing in my eyes.

The soulful beckon of Pachelbel's Canon drew me to the boardwalk. Soft lights encircled the promenade of San Sebastian's beautiful cobblestoned harbour. Pinpricked stars appeared in the heavens glowing high above in the darkness. I stood with the crowd, the warm sea breeze caressing me as I surrendered, weak with the love of life and so alive in the moment, more relaxed and peaceful than I had ever been.

I hadn't always felt so free. A very disciplined and rather a somewhat boring teenager with not even one detention at school, I wore the cloak of responsibility well. In my twenties I had forged for myself a professional career in marketing, establishing financial stability and a future that I took quite seriously. I often lived, it seemed, months ahead of every day - planning, studying, striving, and climbing the corporate ladder. I was single, reasonably affluent, independent, and surrounded by a great group of friends. Yet I ached to know what 'stuff' I was really made of.

On wet, cold wintry nights and on long balmy afternoons, I would read stories of fascinating women, boldly setting out on remarkable solo journeys; Swiss explorer Isabelle Eberhard's diary of her late 19th-century travels through the Sahara desert disguised as an Arab man; Genesta Hamilton and Karen Blixen's extraordinary travels throughout Africa; Shirley MacLaine's soul-searching travels to Bhutan and South America; Robyn Davidson's 1,700 mile camel trek across Australia; Sorrel Wilby's solo three thousand kilometer trek across Tibet, and traverse of the Himalaya; English Buddhist Monk, Vicki Mackenzie's twelve year solo meditation at 13,200 feet in a cave in the Himalaya; Kay Cottee's solo history making Australian sailing voyage around the world on First Lady; Australian mountain climber Brigitte Muir's historical ascent of Mt Everest and the world's Seven Summits. The latter are all my contemporaries, heroines who fired up my dreams.

At twenty six, I yearned to be that type of woman: courageous, independent, and capable. I wanted to inhale the world and test myself to discover what was really behind the comfortable fabric that I had come to wear. I wanted to explore cultures unafraid.

But travelling solo (TS) was an admirable woman, who I feared. As my courage grew, I ventured off in search of her. Those first tinges of dawn's light would find me waking in a third world hotel, dusty campground or mountain side villa surrounded by the sights, sounds and smells of a new culture, a new day, my stomach tense with quiet anxiety and excitement. I searched for her everywhere, listening to her no-nonsense down to earth advice, jealous of her natural beauty, sensible shoes, earthy cotton clothing and wash and wear hair. I marvelled at her ability to speak multiple languages and bargain in foreign markets. I adored her courage to stand up to strangers unafraid and demand what was right and fair. She could be confronting, I was polite; she took risks, I took a raincoat; she lived her truth, I searched for mine; she danced in her own company, I waited to be asked. We argued often. It was a love-hate affair.

TS pushed me into the arms of foreign men, whom I adored. She challenged me to climb snow-capped mountains that I feared, to sail seas that churned my stomach, to dive to fly - to try. To spend my money on experiences, I would never admit to at home. She introduced me to a world of 'can-do' self-discovery.

She travelled with me to many lands and stood by me through frightening and hilarious experiences that I shared with strangers and friends, for even in their midst, she knew me. Travelling with her was an adventure into me, a discovery of strength and trust, of courage and gentleness.

TS was a bitch when trying to find a hotel on a dark foreign street or stranded in a Spanish mountain shack in a storm. But when the hurly-burly was done and we survived the adventure unscathed, her tenacity filled me with awe and adrenaline from having come through it together. She was a hell of a travel buddy! And she became my friend.

Years have passed since that time. I am over twice the age I was and she and I have weathered our years together like old friends. Now when she visits, we both know that a woman's delight is borne from the love of many people and she is just one. But when no-one else is here and evening falls, we share a scotch and coke, a good movie and reminisce on all those passionate memories travelling together that culminated on that warm summer's night in love with life on the promenade in San Sebastian, Spain.

I hope that these stories inspire, entertain and remind us all to follow our dreams unafraid of TS and to delight in each day's trivialities, particularly the unplanned ones, which can be full of surprises.

Juliette

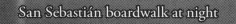

San Sebastián boardwalk at night

Our deepest fear is not that we are inadequate. Our deepest fear is that we are powerful beyond measure. It is our light, not our darkness, that frightens us.

Marianne Williamson: American spiritual teacher,
Author: *"A Return To Love"*

One Spanish Summer

Map of Spain

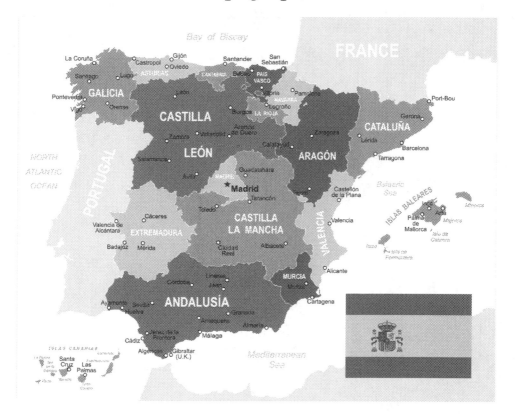

*I see my path, but I don't know where
it leads. Not knowing where I'm going
is what inspires me to travel.*

Rosalia de Castro: Galician writer, poet, 1800's.

Dream
and the way will be clear.
Pray, and the angels will hear.
Leap and the net will appear.

Christine Kane: American singer-songwriter:
"Right Out Of Nowhere"

Leaving Home

You are as powerful and strong as you allow yourself to be. Know that the most difficult part of any endeavour is taking the first step, making the first decision.

Robyn Davidson: Australian adventurer, Author: *"Tracks"*

As Qantas Flight QF81 climbed to 35,000 feet, bound for Singapore, I reclined my seat, threw back a scotch and coke, exhaled slowly, and looked down at the card in my hand, bearing a quotation by the French poet, Guillaunne Apollinaire in the 1800's and hand written by mum.

"Come to the edge" he said.
They came,
he pushed them,
and they flew."

"And so with you Jules" she added before signing off with hugs and kisses. I felt strangely calm but my heart ached and I could see the billowing clouds below becoming blurred from my tears. This was it. I was leaving home alone.

Travelling Solo, (nicknamed TS for short), had taken on a lifelike character of her own over the past year and urged me to take the plunge and face my fears. Leaving home alone, on a one-way ticket was not something I had ever done. Even for a single person with few ties, it can be a strangely unfamiliar behaviour. For me, TS conjured a deep sense of excitement within me that played hide-and-seek with my doubts, fears, and anxiety and questioned my ability to handle the stuff life would throw at me. Yet, contrary to the fears what flurried in my heart, I chose to believe that there is far more to be gained by leaving than by staying. Leaving home took me into dimensions of myself that I never knew existed; staying promised more of the familiar.

Ask anyone who has taken the risk of travelling solo and the answer is usually the same. The decision to go is often harder than the act itself. Tales of my trips were often met with envious eyes and longing exclamations from peers, who had not been able to make that first tough decision. Being single had made my life easier to manage, yet it had brought its own challenges of vulnerability, loneliness and questions of safety where every decision was mine alone. Amidst the pros and cons lie innumerable reasons and excuses why we choose not to make our escape dream a reality. I have always been more afraid of not realizing mine. My stomach still tenses with stress at the thought of regretting what might have been, and some early grey hairs provide testament to my panic.

On board my flight, the movie screens came to life but I turned towards the window. I had left Australia many times before on short adventures, but this time, I was travelling on a one-way ticket. I wanted some time out to shake off the shackles of my well-orchestrated life. Over ten years of career aspirations had moulded me into a corporate, disciplined, task-oriented individual, with characteristics that overflowed into my personal life. I didn't like it. I would need *at least* 10 months off, one for every year of my working life. I wanted to become spontaneous again, to be bilingual, to write, to experience a different culture, live simply, find romance, meet interesting people and throw open the doors of opportunity.

However, such a dream needed courage. As a single woman, loneliness, safety, and financial security were my main concerns. My bank owned my two properties and demanded that I pay my mortgages while away. I resigned from my job, rented out my homes, stored my furniture, sold my car and computer, bought a laptop and portable printer and packed my

Monsack trolley bag. I undertook a basic course in Spanish and took lots of deep breaths.

The thought of escaping to Spain had been born while lying alone in my hospital bed during my convalescence the year before. I thought of it while wondering what I would regret should I not survive or ever regain my full sight. My 'SSST' (Senior Sagittal Sinus Thrombosis, or large blood clot in the head) had resulted from dehydration while on a high altitude trek in Argentina. The clot had caused a build-up of pressure in my head, causing my vision to split into two and my brain to throb with constant migraines that refused to quit. Put a 'P' in front of my 'SSST' and you can begin to appreciate how I felt. Lying around incapacitated wasn't something I took well. From my bed as I watched my world in duplicate, bustle around me, and a throbbing migraine begin to split the base of my skull, I let my mind drift away. So I thought of the things I would miss and regret not having done or the chance to feel again should I not recover. I thought of sunshine and I thought of music and dance and passion, the things in life that fill my spirit. I thought of Spain.

I am romantic and can be quite naive at times. I have no Spanish ancestry. I had only my fantasies from movies, books and songs of olive-skinned, passionate men with black, beckoning, come-hither bedroom eyes and buxom, long, dark haired beautiful Spanish women. I knew of paella and flamenco and arid coastlines with emerald water. I knew of Majorca and Barcelona and Madrid and guitars and siestas. From Hemingway, I knew of Pamplona and bulls and fly fishing in the Pyrenees. I knew of the Spanish love of wine and dancing and all night fiestas and Spanish passion that can so easily turn to aggression. I knew that the Spanish language moved my heart and that was enough. Somewhere inside, I knew that was where I wanted to go, but not as a backpacker this time.

I decided to fly to Spain alone, with no particular set plans, except to study Spanish for the summer and simply live and write and then do what?

"That's the exciting part," TS whispered. *"For once in your life, have the courage to live without being in control of every waking moment."*

3

And one year later, here I was.

Glancing back to my card, I could feel my mum's presence. It was from mum that I inherited my determination and my 'can do' attitude. Mum's belief in me gave me the strength and confidence to follow my heart. Dad's gentle nature reminded me to be kind. A special lunch during my farewell week had allowed us all to share our hopes for my trip. *"You must visit Aranzuez in the stillness of a hot afternoon while listening to 'Concierto de Aranjuez' Dad* had written in my farewell card.

Well into my second drink, I thought of my friends. We were a '30 something' bunch of singles, ex and potential partners, a lovable mixed group of adventurous individuals. Married couples were few but dear. Over the years we had shared overseas adventures to Nepal, India, the Maldives, Sri Lanka, Turkey, Africa and South America. Together, we had skippered 40-foot yachts in the Mediterranean and hiked the Inca trail in Peru. With some I had climbed 5,000-meter peaks, backpacked Europe, explored Australia; snow skied in Austria and Aspen, trucked across the Serengeti and scuba-dived in Fiji. We were young and carefree and had lived and partied together. I loved them dearly; however, now in our thirties, time was moving on and we each knew that those white knights and flaxen-haired maidens may not, for whatever reason, materialize in our lives.

I locked the memory of my family and friends quietly away in my mind and whispered a good-bye, quietly anticipating what the future would bring.

After seven hours of flying, I changed planes in Singapore and waited four hours to catch Qantas QF9 to London. The plane was packed and my anticipation grew as I wondered who would be sitting next to me for the next 13 hours. As I bumped and eased my way down the crowded aisle to seat 47K, I realised that I had drawn the unfortunate middle seat. There would be no escape, to turn unsociably towards the window nor to stretch out into the aisle.

I spotted him before he spotted me. In 47J, a tall, 30-something, brown haired man with a pleasant face travelling alone in the aisle seat.

Next to the window was an elderly grey-haired Englishman. His eyes were already closed with his blow up pillow securely placed around his neck for comfort. Peter, with the pleasant face, turned out to be a geophysicist, who had been working for Santos in Australia. Heavily into the oil industry, Peter had travelled extensively with his work and was returning to his home in England.

As I settled into my seat, we made polite conversation and I realised that trying to stay awake was a hopeless task. My body clock told me it was 2:00 a.m. and simply needed the sleep. As QF9 took off into the night sky, I fell into a deep uninterrupted coma. I cared neither if my head fell carelessly against either of the two nor if my subdued snores would raise their eyebrows.

I awoke eight hours later to the second breakfast sitting of omelette and tomatoes.

Peter was smiling at me. *"You don't have any trouble sleeping on planes, do you?"* he grinned.

The flight from Singapore to London's Heathrow still had four hours to go. Once clean and comfortable, I settled in the in-flight movie. Touchdown, 5.28a.m. London time. Immigration and customs were a breeze and as I walked toward the exit, Peter handed me his card.

"If you ever get into trouble in Spain and need a hand, call me," he said. *"I have lots of friends in Madrid who may be able to help you."*

I pocketed his card with a warm smile and my heart was touched by his generosity. I had simply forgotten the concern and care that travellers often share on the road. Far back in my memory, I could remember such kindness also occurring in other countries, but that seemed a lifetime ago. Too many months of blahhing on the phone and staring at a computer screen had dulled their memory. What else had I forgotten?

As we entered Heathrow's underground walkway, and I dragged my luggage, the drop in temperature suddenly hit me. Ahead, another traveller had stopped to add a few more layers of clothing. We commented on the chill in the air and fell into a conversation. He was also from Australia, a filmmaker going on to Rome that afternoon to work on a new movie. Then, saluting farewell, he called me 'mate' and as he said that, any loneliness I may have felt dissolved in the warmth of that word.

Pulling my luggage, my computer bag in hand, I negotiated the tunnels and stairs and hauled myself onto the empty train to Kings Cross. There I hoped to catch the 8.00a.m. inter-city train to Edinburgh for a one week break before my flight to Madrid. Over the next forty minutes, as the train raced towards the metropolis of London, it slowly filled with sleepy depressed workers enduring severe Monday morning blues. Rugged up against the five-degree chill of morning, they sat or stood, eyes closed or reading papers in their dark grey overcoats and scarves, tired, bored Londoners facing another working week. I, on the other hand, was wide-awake, peering eagerly through the foggy windows to the suburbs beyond, eagerly anticipating what the day would bring.

• • • • • • • • ● • • • • • • • • •

The four hour inter-city train from London to Edinburgh was a joy. On that cold, sunny day the English countryside warmed my heart. The sun streamed through the windows and steam rose from the fields. I dozed lightly, wrapped in my overcoat, lulled by the conversations around me. Two American women, chatting with a bald English gentleman having incredibly long and bony fingers, were swapping travel stories and marvelling at their experiences. I allowed my mind to drift.

It was a familiar feeling to be back in England. I wanted to experience the warmth of friends' company, talk of fascinating things while drinking cocoa and share laughter as the cold afternoons turned to evening. I wanted to stay in the 'now', to admire sunsets, drink good wine, and rediscover the simple joys of life. As the morning wore on, Scotland approached. The countryside turned to fields of green with rolling hills and longhaired, black-nosed sheep stared at me through the foggy windows.

I stood under the railway clock in the Edinburgh station stamping my feet. It was damp and painfully cold. Scottish men, women, and children bustled by me anxiously looking for friends and relatives, all rugged up to the eyeballs. As Eileen approached, I admired her ruddy, warm complexion and her huge smile.

"So there ya are luv, bin waitin long?" My it's cold, isn't it? Here, let me take a bag. My, you've got plenty! My car's over here. There now, in they go. Super!"

Eileen, at fifty-four, was an active, interesting and dynamic woman. She was short, incredibly capable, with vibrant, laughing eyes. Within minutes I was in her car, being whisked off to her home in Dalkeith, a renovated old iron mill in the middle of a beautiful rambling park. Her home, built in the 1700s was fully renovated. It was warm, cosy, and full of colourful rugs and ornaments that she had collected on her travels throughout Africa.

We had met ten years earlier in Crete. That summer we and some others had hiked the Samaria Gorge, drank Greek wine in tiny rambling taverns and walked on isolated beaches enjoyed only by local goat herders. We had kept in contact through the years and now, had many more adventures to share.

As I listened to her wonderful Scottish accent fill the sunny kitchen, my eyes started to close. After traveling for thirty three hours, the jet lag finally got the better of me. I was soon dead to the world.

Scottish spring days can be incredibly cold and it had been snowing lightly. Eileen's brilliantly white, modern kitchen had yellow daffodils and bright red tulips on the counter next to a bowl of fresh fruit. The windows overlooked the park and up-tempo classical music was always playing. What lovely days! Finding a sunny corner in the conservatory, we would sit and chat, exchange stories of our lives, over the past decade and our plans for the future. I listened and laughed to her ongoing saga about her neighbour, problems with the hedge, and the renovations to her lover PJ's cottage on the coast.

The house was adorned with artefacts from all over the world, particularly Africa. She and PJ had travelled to nearly every African country on short escorted tours. Her home reflected her love of adventure travel and African art from such countries as Uganda, Kenya, South Africa, and Tanzania. With an enthusiastic laugh, she showed me an authentic hand-carved African three-legged stool that she had picked up in Uganda in exchange for her black lace bra.

"Miss. Australia, so glad you're home!" beamed Eileen as I entered the kitchen, one day after a short shopping expedition to Dalkeith. With her were two women, and all sat chatting in the kitchen, sharing stories and drinking coffee discussing the drama of the morning. Eileen had taken to calling me Miss Australia and brazenly introduced me as such to all her friends, causing raucous laughter to fill the room. It was not a title that I could hold with a straight face. Stifling their chuckles the two Scottish women sobered up to share how they had found an old man dying from a heart attack in the park whilst walking his dog. They had raced into Eileen's home to telephone for an ambulance. Now that the sad drama had passed, they were sharing how the dog had howled for an hour at the passing of his owner. How tragedy brings strangers together!

On cold afternoons, we poured over photographs on Eileen's gigantic wooden coffee table and lazed on colourful rugs in front of the fire, spending hours re-living our African experiences. Eileen's photographs showed a harsh and dry land, not unlike that of Tanzania, which I had visited in '91. She was a vibrant, intelligent traveller, who discussed her experiences from food to politics. She was full of life and willing to rough it. As I sat and listened to her lively chatter, I marvelled at her knowledge of the places she and PJ had visited. Although I too had been to Africa, my perceptions and the nature of my travel had been sensual, not intellectual. From my expeditions, I remembered wonderful colourful sights, sounds and smells of the Serengeti, of animals, Maasai warriors, burning skies, acacia trees, and mind blowing sunsets, but I knew little of the countries' problems, politics or economics. I had little socio-political knowledge about the illegal ivory trade, the problems caused by borrowings from the World Bank, the unemployment, and exports of the country. I knew absolutely nothing about the changing social fabric of the continent and how it affected the everyday lives of Kenyan and Tanzanian families.

I started to wonder, what kind of traveller had I become? I remembered my first overseas trip to Fiji and how I had read volumes about the country before my departure, eager to learn about another culture. Then, as the trips to strange lands became more frequent, I had researched less and less getting hooked on to the adrenaline of adventure travel experiences. I had changed. I sat up late that night pondering.

• • • • • • • ● ● • • • • • • • •

As the morning of my departure arrived, I was daunted by the thought of lugging thirty kilos of luggage to London and finding accommodation for the night. The thought of re-negotiating the tube and stairs of the underground was not very appealing. My only saving grace was that I could justify all the bulky clothes because it was so very cold.

Arriving in London, I took the plunge and started to enjoy traveling off my income. No backpacker trudging and groaning for me! In my bright cashmere overcoat, I accepted a porter's invitation to carry my luggage, booked accommodation through a booking agency at Kings Cross station and hired a taxi to take me to a hotel in Paddington for the night. *"What the hell"* TS exclaimed! *"Do it with some style at least Jules"* I confess, I do love it when men carry my luggage.

My chosen hotel sounded and looked grand from the outside, but her rooms were simple. It was the first of many decent shoe boxes I would come to sleep in as the year unfolded. At least it was clean and I had my own bathroom. As if by fate, the hotel was full of Spanish tourists and I was tempted to wander down to reception for a chat. However, despite my courageous escape from Australia, the thought of finally chatting to real Spaniards in Spanish left me bashful.

"I can't really say much. I'll sound silly. They probably won't understand me. Who am I trying to kid anyway? I know I'll feel really stupid."

TS sighed and rolled her eyes in exasperation. I never did escape my room that evening. Months later in Spain, when I would recall that night of lost opportunity, I had to smile. Oh! How our fears, like strait jackets, restrict and bind us from taking chances. Psychologically, leaving Australia on a one-way ticket had been a large step for me, which was cushioned only by the warmth of staying with friends in Scotland. Now, I was poised to truly enter the unknown. As I contemplated my upcoming arrival in Madrid, I paced my room, lunging again and again for my Spanish dictionary in an effort to rehearse for the dramas that I anticipated might soon follow.

The next morning found me simmering with quiet anticipation. *"A cab, please,"* I said, *"to the most convenient tube station for Heathrow."* I was quite enjoying the newfound luxury of baggage handlers and friendly taxi drivers and the staff at the front desk were pleased to assist. Before long and to my surprise, a brand new, shiny, grey and very sleek Mercedes with leather seats appeared. The driver leaned across, lowered the electric window and warmly beckoned me toward the cab.

"For me? No, surely not. Are you sure?" I asked, full of cynicism. Albeit, with images of pound notes dancing before my eyes I reluctantly allowed my luggage to be loaded, not sure if I was being taken for a very expensive ride. However, the driver had kind eyes and smiling, he reassured me that the cost would not be exorbitant. He was the brother of the desk clerk. *"Hmmm,"* I thought. As we pulled away from the curb, I realised with dismay that there was no meter in the car. Ducking my questions, instead, my Arabic-English driver focused on how I would like to pay for the trip. He pointed out of course that a Mercedes was not a black cab, we had quadraphonic stereo music, excellent heating, a luxurious interior and I was being chauffeur driven. He offered to take credit card. I felt my heart sink with dismay as I wondered how, with all my years traveling and bartering with cab drivers in third world countries, could I possibly have fallen for this in the center of London. Finally pulling up at the station, the shocking moment arrived.

"How much you pay?" he asked.

"Only as much as a normal cab fare" I answered outwardly, mimicking TS's tenacity and bracing myself, but inside my heart was sinking.

"Alright, five pounds."

His eyes twinkled as his face broke into a wide smile. I gasped and gave him a friendly punch on the arm as I realised with delight that he had been teasing me all along. The pressure disappeared.

I was going to have to loosen up if I was to enjoy this adventure. Now I was ready. At last, after months of dreaming, planning and saving, I felt a new chapter begin.

If you really want to play, lighten your load. TS

Luggage

On a long journey,
even a straw weighs heavy

Spanish Proverb

As I looked around at the arrivals terminal of Madrid International airport, a tall woman leaned expectantly over the barrier and waved to me.

"I hoped I hadn't missed you. You look just like you described yourself!" she said relieved. *"Welcome to Madrid. Is all this luggage yours?"*

Tania was a friend of a friend, someone I had never met or spoken to. Our letters had passed each other in the mail, leaving me with no knowledge of whether she would or could meet me. Tania was also from Adelaide and had left a year before to live in Spain and was now teaching English full time. Her Spanish was impeccable, the result of having a Spanish mother and learning the language from an early age. I was so envious. She expertly guided me to the airport bus and together we headed for the center of town. I followed speechlessly and felt actually relieved by her company.

"I've checked out three hotels for you to choose from," she said, showing me three business cards. *"They're all in the center, right near Puerto Del Sol.*

"The door of the sun - that sounds good," I said as we hailed a cab. How wonderful it was to be met and looked after. I relaxed, realising that I was in safe hands. It's funny how things happen unexpectedly. Who was this

strange woman, who was so helpful so as to go out of her way for me - for someone she didn't know? Why was she looking after me so well? It was just the first of many "gifts" of unexpected friendships, which would arise throughout my Spanish summer - "gifts" which appeared from nowhere when the time was right.

As I settled in my new accommodation, I re-adjusted the small bedside table to make room for my laptop and surveyed my cubbyhole. I had chosen a middle of the price range room with shower to be my home for a few days. If I turned on my heels I could rotate without falling over any luggage. There was little floor space to be seen.

"Oh well," I said as I climbed over "Monsack" my trolley bag, to the door. *"You and I are just going to have to learn to live together,"*. Strange when we are alone, how we let inanimate objects take on human characteristics. Both "Monsack", my travel bag, and "Mongo", my travelling good luck bear, were to become extraordinarily important to me in the months to come, providing me with hours of one-way conversation, only a solo traveller could appreciate.

Tania proved to be an invaluable contact and friend, ushering me here and there, showing me the sights of Madrid and ensuring that I tasted the best tapas the city had to offer. Together we walked miles in the sunshine, as she became my own personal tour guide who gave me the best advice possible. Each night I returned to my cubbyhole and jumped to reach the bed, hidden under days of casual living.

As the week drew to an end, my thoughts returned again to the road. Soon I would have to travel to Salamanca, a historic university town, which was three hours away. But first I would have to get to Chamartin, the regional train station. The thought was again daunting.

I consulted my puny frame. Did this body want to negotiate the Spanish Metro on its own with all this luggage? However, the Metro was very fast, clean and cheap. The metro journey entailed catching two sardine can-like trains, climb twenty seven steps up and thirty four down, plus balance up five escalators and squeeze through two turnstiles for only 135 pesetas (about $1.50). Or maybe I could simply take a taxi for

1,850 pesetas (about $20) and let the taxi driver do all the work? The joys of travelling alone with luggage. My body was not impressed. It really shouldn't have been a hard decision. *"Go on - take the taxi"*, TS pleaded. Before the debate could take hold, my mind was distracted.

The romantic strains of Spanish music filtered through my apartment's open window and interrupted my debating thoughts. Although the afternoon was turning slightly cool, I was reluctant to close it. A woman's voice from a nearby apartment joined in the chorus as she contentedly went about her housework. I relaxed and smiled. The Hostel Alicante in central Madrid had come to feel like home. In the kitchen, my hosts, Sofia and Jose, were chatting in Spanish as they enjoyed a late lunch. The smell of fried capsicums drifted down the passage and the hostel felt alive.

Drawn to the warmth of the kitchen, I was welcomed with a cafe con leche and laughter as I stumbled slightly with my Spanish to discuss my predicament.

As a single woman travelling alone, such safe hostels were a real find. My basic Spanish had comfortably allowed me to negotiate my way around town, but more interesting conversations with locals had been difficult to share. I warmly welcomed Sofia's advice as she warned me, once again to keep my purse close to my body and hold onto my bags, particularly in the Metro. Each night, as I returned from my explorations, she had inquired with genuine concern about my day, listening to my limited vocabulary with the patience only a mother can provide! My Spanish had improved remarkably in just one week because of these chats and the support given by such lovely local people.

Turning the conversation to my predicament, I asked their advice. Jose frowned and then exclaimed as he remembered something. *"Chamartin el sábado? No te precupes. Vamos juntos en coche!"* (Chamartin on Saturday? No problem - we go together in my car!) We laughed out loud and toasted on another cafe con leche. My daunting thoughts evaporated into thin air. One week in Spain and I had been wrapped in cotton wool by strangers who had bent over backwards for me. Their concern and assistance had staggered me. Would I have been so welcoming? *"Remember this,"* I thought. I could feel a new rhythm of unexpected kindness smiling on my life.

Savour each exquisite bite.
Let's get drunk
on Spanish life. TS

Life in a 'Piso'

Lighten up.
Learn to have fun with your tongue. TS

"*Calle de San Claudio por favor,*" I said, leaning toward the front seat of the cab and concentrating on rolling my 'r's. It was a cold April afternoon and Salamanca's train station was busy. I was keen to get out of the weather, find my accommodation and meet my host family.

"*Donde?*"

"*Calle de San Claudio*" I repeated.

"*Vale, vale, vale.*" He replied OK and I realised I had been understood.

Doña Louisa's strong enthusiastic voice vibrated through the intercom in Spanish and I heard her push the security buzzer. The door swung open and I dragged my luggage into the marble reception hall of her 'piso', or new apartment block.

I had expected a small, dark, comfortable down market home of a poorer family. I had expected a large jolly buxom señora to welcome me. I had wanted to be drawn into a large, happy, family lifestyle with lots of teenage kids coming and going and a grumpy father who spoke no English. Oh, television and movies! What scenes and visual memories they create! My naiveté was showing.

Doña Louisa was a short, attractive, single, vibrant woman with straight, blond, bobbed hair that was so popular in Spain. So much for my expectations about olive-skinned, long dark-haired, buxom Spanish women. Wearing blue jeans and a well-fitting long sleeved "t" shirt that showed off her trim figure, she enthusiastically showed me my room, which was to be my home for the next three months. Soon I realised that she didn't speak a word of English and my beginner's Spanish was soon stretched to the limit.

Doña Louisa's apartment was small but boasted of new and upmarket furniture. It consisted of three bedrooms, an open space dining and lounge room, a galley kitchen and a sparklingly clean bathroom. The parquetry floors were polished and covered with large rugs. In the lounge room, the glass-topped coffee table was clear of fingerprints and flowers added colour to the small but comfortably furnished room. Her lounge suite faced a French polished wall-unit to store the television, stereo, books, records, and photos. In fact, everything glistened and shone. Sliding doors from the lounge room and kitchen opened onto a tiny balcony, large enough to place a clothes' horse. The view looked into dozens of other apartments lining the street.

My room, like the rest of the apartment, was comfortable, modern and clean, with parquetry floor and a large blue rug. A generous window offered a view of the suburban street below. My single bed was draped with a bright blue quilt with a small bedside table and lamp placed nearby. The built-in wardrobe provided all the space that I needed for my luggage. There was a small round wicker glass topped table with white lace tablecloth and a wicker chair. The entire frame of the large rectangular mirror on my bedroom wall was soon adorned lovingly with photos of the home.

Tired from my 3-hour train trip from Madrid, I sank onto the bed and rested, momentarily taking in my surroundings. I was surprised that the room was so comfortable and pleased that the university had chosen this particular home for my billet.

I was eager to shower and get into warm and comfortable clothes, so I inquired with my broken Spanish, if I could use the bathroom. I was enthusiastically provided with a tour of the tiny room. The hot water tap was on a different switch and had to be turned on prior to bathing, so she invited me to tell her, whenever I required a bath. She would then turn the switch in the kitchen for me. She also showed how to rinse the bath when I would finish and how to re-hang the bath mat and towels neatly in their allotted spot. I spent a wonderful fifteen minutes enjoying a hot shower and completed the tasks required of me, before returning to my room to get changed.

But before I could change into anything, a tap at my door soon brought to my attention a very concerned Doña Louisa. She took me by the hand and led me sternly back to the bathroom. Although I could not understand a word she said, her tone made it quite clear that as she did not have an exhaust fan, steaming up the bathroom was entirely unacceptable. The steam would affect the mirror and ceiling paint and I was not to have such hot showers in the future. Then, leaving me standing there in my towel, she disappeared into the lounge room, shaking her hands in the air in apparent desperation. My indoctrination was over. She had asserted her position, stated the rules and shown me who the boss was. I repressed a smile and returned quietly to my room, intrigued by the emotional scene that had just been played.

It didn't take me long to realise that Doña Louisa was just a little obsessive-compulsive when it came to her home and that she took enormous pride in her material possessions. This was to cause me some angst in the successive months as I battled to abide by the dozens of rules she required us to live by.

To my relief, I wasn't alone in my challenge. That same day, the front door opened with a whirl of energy. It was the freckled, smiling and enthusiastic face of Kate from bedroom number three, gesturing for me to follow her. We entered her room whereon she took both my hands in hers and mischievously whispered, *'I am so glad you have arrived! Welcome to la vida loca!! (the crazy life!)*

Then she stifled a laugh and bringing her index finger to her lips, very quietly closed her bedroom door and pulled me to sit down with her on the bed. Her face was very enthusiastic and welcoming and I took an instant liking to her. From that moment on, we became friends. English was not to be spoken in the homes of our host families, so she suggested we escape the apartment to share our news and get to know each other. Once out of the house, our conversations never ebbed.

Kate was in her early twenties, from South Carolina. She was studying Spanish as part of her degree and was spending the summer in Spain to brush up on her language skills. She had been in Salamanca for a month already, living alone with Doña Louisa, and was nearly at her wit's end. Luckily, she had come to Spain with other student friends, billeted to different families so she spent a lot of time out of the house. Regardless, the month had been quite a challenge and Kate simply burst with laughter telling me her tales of woe.

Doña Louisa was a fascinating, unforgettable woman and at forty seven years of age, she looked wonderful. Divorced, she had managed to secure a level of income and comfort that she needed. She loved crossword puzzles, tabloid magazines, and soap operas. Like many Spaniards, she attended mass every Sunday, smoked and was exceptionally well groomed. She owned wonderfully expensive clothes and ensured that her nail polish and shoes matched her outfits.

A beautician, she no longer needed to work due to her settlement. Students such as Kate and I provided her with the pocket money she required, although as the weeks rolled on, she made it quite clear that our board was just not high enough. I was in agreement. In fact, the billeting arrangements charged by the university were very reasonable. We paid the equivalent of just thirty dollars per day for room and three meals.

I was soon to experience the first of these meals as our 2:00p.m. lunch was not far away. Smiling, we returned to the apartment. Kate glanced at the bathroom indicating that washing before lunch was expected. I followed the rules, ensuring I left the towels very neatly hung and not a speck in the basin.

Spaniards eat a three-course lunch, the main meal of the day. It usually begins with a soup or light salad followed by a hot meal and is finished off with fruit or yogurt. Like many Spaniards, Doña Louisa enjoyed cooking copious amounts of fried food. Olive oil is as staple to a Spaniards diet as milk and bread are to Australians. Over the weeks, we enjoyed empanadas, lightly fried calamari and chips, pork chops and chips, crumbed and fried chicken and chips, chicken paella, conchettas, hard boiled eggs with mayonnaise and shredded lettuce, ham and cheese sandwiches, tortillas and wonderful homemade soups, pizzas and pasta dishes...and chips.

Despite all the fried food, Doña Louisa proved to be a great cook and bright and entertaining company. As she served us our meals, she talked non-stop with animated, exaggerated expressions. Her genuine laugh was loud and hearty. Although I could understand little of what she said, her expressions were more than adequate, providing clues as to when I should nod and smile. In truth, for the first few weeks, I had little idea what she talked about and Kate was left to carry on the conversation for both of us.

I was often helped along by Kate's appropriately timed kicks from under the table and raised eyebrows and stares at my offending behaviour whenever my elbows would creep onto the table. In fact, whenever Doña Louisa's back was turned, Kate sent me sign language, messages that saved me from our senoras wrath on many occasions.

"Always keep your door closed when you are in your bedroom; turn off the light and close your door when you leave your room; don't make any noise before 9:00am in the morning; take your shoes off at the front door; don't read in the lounge room; don't hang any wet things in your bedroom; only have one shower per day; be as silent as air when entering the house at night; don't sit on the floor to watch TV; don't use the stereo; don't even try to get away with turning the hot water on yourself; don't use the telephone; ask if you want anything out of the fridge; don't drink in the lounge room.

The list went on and on. Many times I was caught red handed and suffered a torrent of angry exclamations. Walking to the university together after lunch, Kate and I would often laugh about our failings together. There was never a dull moment.

However, whenever Kate wasn't around, life took on a more sobering tone, especially in those early weeks. Language restrictions made conversations with Doña Louisa very limited. I could not understand the television, radio or read newspapers or magazines, even though I persisted in trying to understand the spirit of what I saw and heard. After a couple of weeks, as my ear adapted to the rhythm of the language, I found myself picking up enough words to gain more than just a gist of what was going on in the evening news. Even so, in those first few weeks, there were times when I found myself wrapped for warmth in my overcoat in my room, tears in my eyes and feeling cold and as isolated as I have ever felt in my life. Letters from home were devoured and I missed my family and friends more than ever and the world became a smaller place.

I found that many things I had grown to take for granted over the years were discounted in this new environment. In Australia I had been the manager of a department and was responsible for a team of people, budgets with results to achieve. Consequently, I had grown used to a respectful diplomacy when speaking with others. While in Spain, I was a student and treated as one. My positional power was no more.

Generally speaking, Spaniards are very direct, passionate people who say what they mean. It's a characteristic which I admire but took some time to become used to. One day while chatting with Doña Louisa in the galley kitchen while she prepared lunch, I leaned on the wall as I tried to remember a word I needed to use.

"Por favor Julietta!!!" she exclaimed in anger at my slack posture and proceeded to shoo me out of the kitchen before wiping down the wall and grumbling to herself about that Australian girl! I left her to it, the conversation long forgotten. I realized there was no diplomacy when being spoken to by Doña Louisa and her tone left little to the imagination! I felt like a scolded child.

I was forced to reflect on how comfortably I had allowed myself to be cocooned by the environment given to me by my employment over the years! You take away the position of management and once again we are all on even terms, to be judged not by what we have achieved but by who we are as people. It was a humbling experience to become aware of my own ego.

However, the situation needed handling and I decided that if I could not stand to be treated as a six-year-old, I would need to change my approach and learn how to manage this difficult woman. I knew that if I gave Doña Louisa exactly what she wanted, I could strategically win her over until she was eating out of my hand. I began to watch her closely while pondering on the best approach to take. I soon found the key. She loved compliments.

Doña Louisa had many saving graces. She was never moody for long. She had a wonderful hearty laugh that was very engaging. She was exceptionally patient with me as I struggled to learn her language and she was a full on party animal. At forty seven, the woman had stamina. It was nothing for her to go out on the town one or two nights a week and come home at dawn. She loved smoky bars, alcohol, and good music, and she loved to laugh, smoke and sleep late. I absolutely loved this side of her and decided it was best to be in her good books. My plan was sealed. I would counter attack with genuine apologies whenever I upset her and overwhelm her with compliments whenever possible.

Even Kate began to notice and commented on my positive attitude toward Doña Louisa. I was determined that the woman would not get me down, and Kate vowed to back me up. I became overbearingly nice and Doña Louisa lapped it up. Slowly, the reprimands began to subside.

Life was on an upward trend and continued to get better and better. My language skills improved and I began to join in the conversations at the dinner table. On more than one occasion, both Kate and Doña Louisa burst into laughter at my inappropriate use of words but I was improving. One day, as I was describing a man I had seen in town, both of them put down their cutlery and looked at me in amazement. Apparently, I had finally said a whole paragraph without one grammatical error.

Kate had introduced me to both her circle of friends and a wonderful laundromat. Together we shared movies, concerts, walks along the river, dinners and parties. She continued to be a positive and happy spirit despite the day-to-day chastising she received from Doña Louisa.

Her departure back to the US in early June was a sad affair. I knew I would really miss our shared laughs and moans over Doña Louisa's rules. Her last night in Salamanca was a dawn buster with her American friends who all stayed up to watch the sunrise before heading to catch the train to Madrid. As we crept into the apartment at 6.00am, to pick up her things, we shared a big hug and exchanged tears, gifts, and addresses. I helped her to her taxi and waved her off. Sunrise is such a sad time to wave someone good-bye. As for me, another day was dawning and I still had a lot of Spain to look forward to.

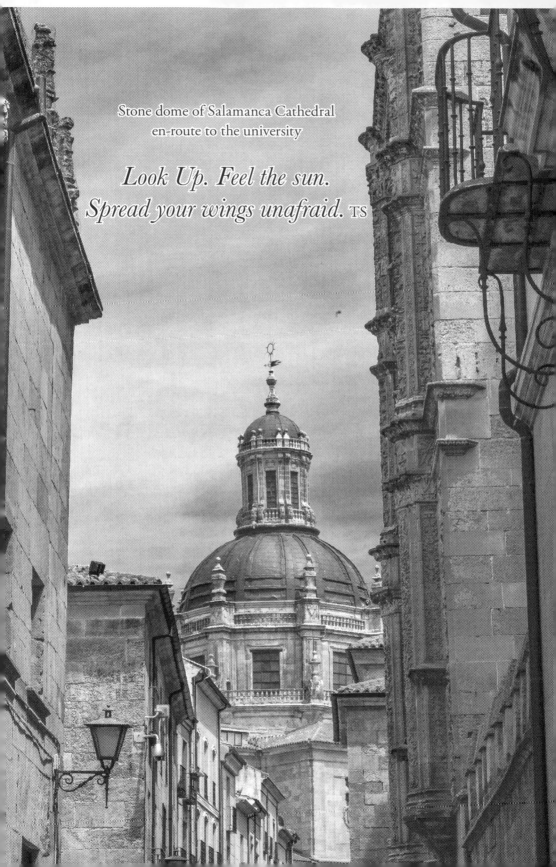

Stone dome of Salamanca Cathedral
en-route to the university

Look Up. Feel the sun.
Spread your wings unafraid. TS

Where Ancient Truths
and Storks Are

Taking time out to be still and think is often a better investment for future productivity than cramming every waking moment with feverish activity.

Vicki Mackenzie: British Buddhist Nun. Author: *"A Cave in the Snow"*

Shielding my eyes from the sun, I squinted, searching the parapets as I listened to the tourist's excited comments.

"There to the left. She's above the bell tower. She'll move in a moment"

What was it? I could see the silhouette – a large outline of something – a nest? Surely not one so large or so high. Within a few moments, the white breast and long black-tipped wings of the largest stork I had ever seen stepped carefully within view. Balancing on the edge of the cathedral dome, she lifted her enormous wings and with one slow movement she stepped into mid-air. Rising higher, she majestically soared over me, an eclipse of the sun, a silent slow moving shadow and then she was gone.

Inquisitively, enthralled I walked to the far side of the cathedral and scanned the parapets again. There it was. Perched at the summit of one dome was the nest, over four feet wide. The perfect vantage point to survey the city.

It seemed wonderful that Salamanca, one of Spain's most beautiful cobble-stone cities, and famous for the oldest, most prestigious university in Spain, should have storks watching over it. For centuries, since 1218, this city near the border of Spain and Portugal has been an intellectual centre for students, scholars, and royals interested in philosophy, literature, scientific learning and education. Hundreds of prominent Spanish intellectuals throughout history have trodden its university halls, once considered to be as important as the Universities of Bologna, Paris, and Oxford, 'the four leading lights' of the medieval world.

That year, 1996, over 30,500 students attended lectures in its grand stone-walled faculties, contemplated in its cobble patios and cloisters, and walked its narrow winding streets. Three-month intensive language courses attracted 3,500 extranjeros - students from America, Japan, Germany, and France. They came to study Spanish in the *"Courses Internationales,"* Spain's most famous international language faculty and submerge themselves in Spanish life. As one of only a handful of Australian students, I could not help wonder why we were so under-represented.

"Australia, phew! Es muy lejos!" (Very far!) was our constant greeting.

"Si, es muy lejos." Unlike the hundreds of Americans, who came in groups from universities around America, the few Australian students I met were solo independent travellers like myself and very far from home.

It was a hot Saturday afternoon and the old city of Salamanca with its breathtakingly large central square of Plaza Mayor, the cathedral grounds, and patios, were full of tourists. However, something about the stork had aroused my interest. Encouraged by TS to go exploring, I made my way past a group of German tourists, turned up Calle Latina Tavia and took the shortcut to the university to find a better vantage point.

The sculptured entryway of the university rises majestically and is apparently one of the best examples of Spanish Plateresque style in all of Spain. It's most intriguing feature for tourists and students alike, is the simple carved image of a small frog on top of a human skull that lies teasingly camouflaged above the doors. It is said to represent the darkness of prison life, and if found without help, is expected to bring great luck in exams and marriage within a year. A large group of Japanese tourists was excitedly scanning the archway, searching for the frog, their cameras poised in expectation. Local Spaniards were offering advice for a small fee when the neck pain becomes too great.

The stone statue of Fray Luis de Leon, one of the most respected literati of the golden age also guards the university's entrance. I pardoned my way through the noisy throng, past Fray Luis, hoping to find a stairway to the roof for a better view. On entering the dark, cold university cloister, silence descended and I suddenly stepped back into history.

Each wood-panelled gigantic study room, filled with sturdy, polished wooden pews, was silent and dark. Enormous heavily carved pulpits towered overhead, from which lecturers once shared their wisdom. Ancient tapestries draped the walls of every room.

I slowly climbed the grand stone staircase to the first floor overlooking the rectangular cloister below. The ancient library, like a tomb, was silent, a museum, sealed by a beautiful 16th-century iron gate. Entranced, I peered through the bars. What thoughts lay captured in the hundreds of ancient, leather-bound books that lined its rich Baroque bookcases? What knowledge filled the hundreds of rare and exquisite pages from all the faculties of Spain? What spirits escaped from their pages at night and played behind the eyes of the enormous portraits that lined the walls? What famous scholars, philosophers and professors had sat in these dark cloisters, endlessly contemplating philosophy, love, and literature and had lectured in these grand halls over the centuries? I was captivated.

A long warm shaft of sunlight played teasingly at my feet from the open-roofed cloister. Looking up, the cathedral was now in full view. Between the stone arches, I could see the cathedral's majestic dome shining in the late afternoon sun. Fascinated, I wanted to see the stork again. She drew me, full of wonder, to marvel at her size, freedom, and grace. She was there, closer now. As I watched in wonder, she rose to welcome her mate, returning to the nest. Two intimate and graceful creatures crooning in the late afternoon sunshine, so high above all the hustle and thirst for truth far below. They nuzzled. TS smiled.

Note to Self…..

Get some lovin!

Let's dance on the table.
Let's embrace the night.
Let's sing until dawn
with our arms entwined. TS

A Student's Life

Let us step into the night and pursue
that flighty temptress, adventure.

J.K. Rowling: British Author: *"Harry Potter and the Half Blood Prince"*

It had been fourteen years since I had been a full-time university student. Though, I was surprised that so little had changed, a tremendous lifestyle shift was about to grab and shake me by my thirty-something collar. Having worked in the corporate world for over ten years and mingled with a somewhat older crowd, I was keen to enjoy this younger scene.

Students seem to be bound inextricably together in a surreal existence of lectures, tutorials, practicals and library hours. This is mixed intermittently with long periods of drinking coffee in cafes, beer in bars, sun-baking and last minute homework. Throughout the world, regions may change but the story changes little.

The University of Salamanca was slightly different. It was one of the oldest in Europe and exceedingly beautiful. English was not to be spoken. Our class boasted of six nationalities and I was ten to fourteen years older than most students. The 3,500 foreign students who tramped the universities cobblestone patios and halls that summer, also danced in the taverns and discos every night. Most were billeted to local families who made their living feeding and lodging students and rarely saw their lodgers. The cycle of student life allowed for maximum time outside homes and classrooms to experience the language of the city.

Classes were from 4.00p.m. - 8:00p.m. each evening. Dinner with host families was eaten at 10:00p.m. Nightlife lasted from midnight to dawn. Breakfast was at 10:00a.m. and lunch at 2:00p.m. Cafes, movies, concerts, excursions and homework filled the in-between hours and so the cycle continued day after day. It was like waking up in a wonderland where everything was running two hours later than usual, where everything moved to a different rhythm and the long hot summer stretched out ahead of us. We had everything to look forward to. By the height of summer, life seemed extraordinarily perfect.

The first few weeks of April however, were very cold. The first day we sat for initial grammar and conversation tests, where we were graded and bonded together for the next three months, strangers from all over the world.

We would arrive for classes rugged against the winds that raced through the alleyways of Salamanca and shiver in the outdoor Patio de Escualas in our breaks. The Europeans would drag on cigarettes, the Americans would gulp coffee. There were many Americans, particularly from California, Georgia, Virginia, North and South Carolina, and Texas. The southern United States was well represented and the southern accent rang daily through the corridors.

"Hey y,'all – howya doing?"

'Hey girl didn't see ya last night! Howya bin?'

"Oh man, my fu....g head.

You shoulda bin there bro, it was wild."

The age gap was very apparent to me. What was this strange American southern dialect? I was going to have to tune into their accent and adapt to their colourful vocabulary.

The university had cleverly targeted American university students for the April - June intake, all of whom were studying Spanish as part of their degree. Many of the students came in pairs with friends and were billeted to local families. Two female students, Jamie and Ashley from Georgia, became my close companions. By spending the summer in Spain, they gained credits toward their degree and had a fabulous holiday. Most of the American students were rich, young and full of life and laughter. The girls wanted to shop, the guys wanted to drink and they all wanted to party. Mum and dad were paying most of their bills and life was unbelievably good.

However, not all students had the luxury of being sponsored by their parents and holidaying with their friends. Other students from all over Europe and Asia such as Shigeko from Japan, Ingrid from Czechoslovakia, Lars and Oliver from Germany and Joanna and myself from Australia, were studying for the joy of it. We were there to broaden our language skills; travelling alone and paying for the privilege ourselves. Other, such as Farook and Saquib, from the Pakistan foreign office, were being sponsored by their government with a view to being posted to the Pakistan embassies of Madrid, Buenos Aries or Mexico City.

Having studied conversational Spanish in Australia, I could understand and share very simple conversations with local people, however my written grammar skills were non-existent. As the initial grading tests were written comprehension, I was not surprised to fail miserably. I found myself in *"El Español Basico,"* the basic Spanish class, learning about the ongoing adventures of three fictional students, Martin, Paul, and Claudia.

Shami, a tiny petite Californian with long, straight, brown hair, lots of energy and a mischievous streak, was great fun and we quickly formed a close alliance. Unlike our classmates, who were all beginners, Shami and I could at least understand and exchange a few words with our teacher Don Juan, who teasingly chose to speak no English at all.

Whispering secretly and passing answers to others when Don Juan's back was turned became a fine-tuned art that I thoroughly enjoyed. Perhaps my dream of landing a detention at school would be fulfilled before the summer was through.

Don Juan was a wonderful teacher. A kind and patient man in his thirties, he was married with children. He loved his work and because of his interaction with international students he had a wonderful knowledge of the history of many countries and often put his students to shame. His personal challenge was to teach us to understand and speak Spanish without ever speaking a word of English himself. By drawing pictures on the blackboard and by acting out scenarios in the classroom he would enunciate, exaggerate, and double us over with laughter as he taught us how to read the Spanish body language of the streets. An ongoing game of charades was played, filling our classroom with laughter. We learned quickly.

This was not the case with our other lecturer Doña Katerina. Our four hours of study every day consisted of two hours classroom work with Don Juan and two hours laboratory work with Doña Katerina. She was a young, attractive Spanish woman who often had the young stud male students drooling over her and making remarkable fools of themselves. Unfortunately, Doña Katerina could understand no English at all, spoke Spanish very quickly and left their courageous flirtatious attempts floundering.

After two hours with Don Juan we were often in a far too playful mood to get serious with Doña Katerina.

Reluctantly, under her more stern approach to study, we would sit in semi-isolated booths and listen to conversations on headphones that used vocabulary we had been learning in the classroom. We would then write the answers to questions about the conversation to see how much we had understood. The technique was excellent for building listening and comprehension skills but it was far more entertaining to watch the young studs failing in their flirtatious attempts to win her favour.

After class, students would head for the magnificent Plaza Mayor in the old city and huddle in cafes for hours, drinking strong cafe con leches, sharing laughs, homework and planning the night ahead. TS was an annoyance, and I tried to resist her attempts to push me beyond my comfort zone, preferring to surround myself in loneliness in those first few weeks. Shami and I had bonded from the start but she lived across town and because of the biting cold weather, there was little to do between classes except sit in my room and read for hours in my self-absorbed exile, feeling sorry for myself.

By May, with the approach of summer, the weather warmed. I awoke early to explore Salamanca's cafes and indulge myself for hours observing life in Plaza Mayor's paved patios. TS was becoming easier to be with and she would often share my table with comfortable familiarity. The café chairs at that early hour in the cool of the morning were all neatly stacked. By 8.00a.m. the first Spanish students would arrive on foot passing through the Plaza on their way to 9.00a.m. classes at the Universidad. By 10.00a.m. some chairs would be erected. By 2.00p.m. hundreds of chairs and tables would all be occupied by tourists. Then, as the afternoon wore on, wave after wave of students descended from the Universidad, strolled casually into the Plaza and the entertainment really began. By 7.30p.m. it was standing room only and the Plaza would come alive with music, conversation, laughter, local children playing, mothers with strollers bumping over the cobbled paving, chairs scrapping as people sat, stood, argued, laughed, sang and came and went in an never ending procession that would continue into the early hours.

As the weather warmed, layers of clothing were shed. The birds were singing and the breezes had turned into gentle caresses. Beautiful people have a way of glowing with life and hope. The warmer weather brought many of the female students breezing into class with bare, brown mid-drifts with pierced navels. Slim legs, long flowing straight shiny hair, clear complexions and dazzling white teeth. They looked so glamorous.

Pre-class coffee sessions moved al fresco (in the open air) into the Plaza Mayor with better sun tanning options. Homework was done in the sunshine drinking iced tea. Sunglasses were brought out and buskers appeared. After class, coffees chats extended to pre-dinner tapas and drinks. Families gravitated to the Plaza Mayor; adults started taking their parents on evening strolls and children stayed out late laughing and playing in the warm air.

On warm afternoons and evenings I often met with my "Intercambio" (language buddy) to practise my Spanish. Paquita was Spanish, married with two beautiful young children and was keen to improve her English. She lived in Salamanca and we would meet socially to chat and help each other understand local words and their meaning in Spanish and English. What began as polite café conversations soon turned into fun shopping expeditions, cooking classes, long walks and play dates with her children as we took turns alternating between our native tongues, teaching each other the language of the street. We laughed so much at our initial misunderstandings and misinterpretations but we were soon able to converse well. We both improved enormously and became good friends.

Summer nights began to explode into party mode. Twenty-four hour bars, sangria, tapas and open flirtations. Life was free, the nights were warm, music was plenty and we danced until dawn. In Australia, I was usually in bed by 10.30p.m. in preparation for 8.30a.m. meetings at the office. I was used to dinner parties with friends and after work drinks with suits. My curiosity was aroused. Could I adapt to this scene? With TS's encouragement, my chameleon returned.

"I'll meet you at 11.30pm chica, below the clock" was the familiar call as classes ended each day. There were bars, clubs, cafes, dozens and dozens of them, and music poured from everyone until dawn. The most popular bars catered for the hundreds of American sorority and fraternity "90210ers" who spilled over onto the pavements' night after night spinning American top forty CD's nonstop.

We would visit "Submerino"; "Puerto de Chus" and "Cafe Moderno" which became our regular nocturnal haunts. First stop was usually "El Litro bar" because the beer was cheap, a very popular watering hole for many of the guys on warm summer nights. Not much of a beer drinker, I managed one and then two or even three pints as a warm up before heading off to dance. As the weeks passed, we started to explore new streets, bars and clubs offering more variations. The party atmosphere never seemed to end. "La Capitan Haddock's" attracted an older Spanish crowd and played jazz and blues. "The Sabor," was full of Latin Americans, who partied all night to traditional sambas and rumbas. "El Balcon" was rocking locals to modern contemporary Spanish top forty and "Camelot" played 50's/60's rock and roll in the early hours before dawn.

On Tuesday nights, "La Biblioteca" (The Library Bar) was packed to the rafters. Low, dark and loud, the books lining its walls literally fell from their shelves as the bar throbbed to the latest House music. There was a clever catch. Squeezing through the throng, students could flip heads or tails for their drinks. If they won, no charge. Exhilarated whoops of excitement resounded before being drowned in that smoky haze. During those first dawn busters, getting home in the early hours was a whole new experience for me.

It was one of those euphoric days and I had danced until 4.00a.m and the bar was still packed. My camarero (waiter) had bought me my share of free drinks and I was ready to leave. I politely rejected his passionate offer to drive me home. Through the throng of dancers in the Submerino bar, I caught Shami's eye.

"I'm off" I intimated. Her bare midriff, slim frame slid toward me.

"Had enough?" she yelled above the techno beat.

"Si, gracias chica. Hasta luego"

"Get a taxi, eh! Don't walk on your own" Her words bounced away.

"Salamanca is very safe at all hours. I can easily walk - no te preocupes" (don't you worry)." I called back, remembering Doña Louisa's advice.

Her home was a mere 10-minute walk from the town center. I respected her advice but I trusted my TS instincts. If I can get a cab, I will, I promised myself.

I spied the exit through the smoke and stepped into the street alone. The cool night air was so refreshing that I was suddenly wide awake but I was out of luck. Dawn rush hour had not begun and the taxi rank outside the Plaza Mayor was yet to fill with cabs. After the throb of the bar, the silence of early morning sounded eerie to me. Preferring not to stand alone in the dark, I decided to walk, hoping to soon flag down an approaching cab.

City women walking alone at night are aware of the tension and quickening throb of their heartbeat while listening to footsteps echoing against empty pavements. I zipped my leather jacket and made sure my money was secure and my arms were free to ward off surprise attacks. There were no taxis in sight.

A dog barked far off as I made my way up Calle Sancti Spiritus, an uphill climb. My breathing was heavier now; my lungs struggling against the smoke from the bar, which still clogged my once pure Australian lungs.

As I turned the corner, into the main street Paseo de Canalejas, it seemed deserted. I was leaving the hub of the town center. I wished my heels were rubber soled so I could slink quietly past any strangers lurking in the shadows. The road was empty. I turned out of Paseo De San Antonio, the last downhill stretch. Behind me, across the street, a middle-aged man appeared alone under the streetlight and continued in my direction. This did not seem good. I remembered my friend's scribbled words on my farewell card:

"You are so strong but you like all of us are so vulnerable. Please, take care of yourself first before anything or anyone else"

Thirty paces behind me, the stranger sniffed loudly. Was he catching up with me? Was I thinking too much? I couldn't tell. I moved to the center of the road where the lights were brightest and, turning into my street ran the last few meters to the entrance of my apartment, my heart beating quickly. I knew better, but the options seemed few.

I came to realise later that my fears were unfounded. Over those wonderful summer months, we learned that Salamanca was indeed very safe. Soon we overcame our initial fears, which we had brought with us from our big and often violent cities. As the weeks passed, I often walked home alone in the pre-dawn hours, and came to relish the quietness of the dark city streets, that had once filled me with useless anxiety.

Adapting to the different rhythm of life and encouraged by TS, I danced more and more until often the night became morning. Then yawning, we would visit early morning cafes and sample "churros," sweet freshly fried bread curls, to be dunked in thick hot chocolate, a specialty of Spain. Laughing merry groups of young student men, plastered with arms around each other, would sing to the dawn. We marvelled at our stamina, cherishing the thought that the months stretched out ahead and there was ample time and friendships to do it all again and again.!

• • • • • • ●● ● ●● • • • • • •

"Alfredo's dead?"

There had been whispers throughout the student quadrangle and cloisters all morning.

"No, it can't be true. What happened last night?"

"No, it was this morning...just a few hours ago.

"Tony was there."

The 4.00p.m. classes were just about to begin but as everyone filed into the faculty buildings the rumours continued. There were whispers that offered pieces of a dramatic but uncertain story, of a fall, an ambulance ride. But no-one seemed to know for sure.

"He fell and hit his head."

"No, I heard he had a heart attack."

"He was a big drinker. I saw him last night about 2.00a.m. and he was drinking... He was well on his way man...."

Before class, Jamie, Ashley and I sat drinking coffee with Lars, a student from Germany. Somehow he had escaped hearing the rumours and looked confused when Jamie raised the subject.

"What are you talking about? Who is it that has died?" asked Lars in his thick German accent, his eyebrows knitted together in concentration.

"That Italian guy, Alfredo. He had dark hair; about twenty three years old...He used to drink at the Litro Bar. He was working on a construction site I heard...had a really young girlfriend but the police can't get in touch with her or his family because no-one knows where he lived." Jamie said quietly.

Lars's face went white.

"What is it?" Ashley asked.

"I know this guy. He lives in the room next to mine. I only saw him last night before I went out. He's a great guy. Helped me move into my room, showed me around, and lent me his computer...."

His voice trailed off. Lars was pale and silent.

"Tony just walked by" Ashley offered. *"He was there. Let's ask him."*

Lars jumped up and left the cafe while the three of us waited quietly, privately knowing the worst. The rumours had been true.

Alfredo was often seen drinking at the Litro Bar with his girlfriend, mixing with students and laughing at the world. He was in his early twenties and worked in Salamanca on a construction site. I saw him most nights and had danced and laughed with him. He was a jovial guy, always happy, with his arm around his best friend, another Italian, teasing all the girls and each other. Together they would drink themselves into oblivion, as young men are often prone to do.

He died just before dawn. He simply fell and couldn't get up. A heart attack? A cracked scull? Alcohol poisoning? The answer was never divulged to the students who raised the alarm and accompanied him by ambulance to the hospital. He died twenty minutes later. For twenty-four hours no one knew where he lived or how to contact his parents or girlfriend. However, all the students knew he was gone.

With the tragedy, a darkness came over the Courses Internationales campus. I felt sick and was teary eyed for two days. In a deep place, the vulnerability that TS showed me filled me with reverence for my life.

Each moment is a gift, requiring choices that determine the quality of our journey. I didn't want to live cautiously with fear, a raincoat and a parachute. My heroines were courageous, independent women, capable of exploring cultures unafraid. It was time to remember my chosen path. TS was teaching me to tread it wisely.

A woman who can stamp her foot and still seduce a man is a woman to be reckoned with. TS

Las Fiestas!

*To party, dance and sing with local people on
every continent is a worthy pursuit.* TS

It is when the sun shines that the eyes and faces of Spaniards,
quickly soften into relaxed smiles. It is a culture that seems to live for
the fiesta, for holidays and for love. It is a culture that does not tame
their desire for singing, for dancing and for the uninhibited celebration
of life itself.

In the summer months, inhibitions disappear from young to old, from
rich to poor. The warm days bring out the exhibitionist in nearly every
Spanish heart.

One such elated summer evening, in the center of the Plaza Mayor,
two talented drummers began striking a slowly intertwined rhythmic
beat. A passing elderly couple, with their faces lined with a lifetime
of struggle, put down their parcels. Hand in hand, they stepped into
the center of the on-looking crowd. They faced each other and then
began a seductive, sensual dance. Slowly, the old man raised his hands
to shoulder height and began to click his fingers. Their eyes locked.
Never ceasing to distract their gaze from each other, they moved slowly
in unison, their footsteps moving backwards and forwards together as

one. As if mesmerised, another couple joined them, then another and another until over a dozen passers-by were moving as one line, clicking their fingers, and swaying in the night to the rhythm. Throughout Spain, it is as natural as eating and drinking. To dance is to celebrate life itself.

There were many one day fiestas throughout those summer months. We had little idea of their significance or origin and little did it matter. No classes for us meant play and in the Plaza Mayor, large sound stages were often erected for concerts and live music. As the weather became hotter, the music would start later and later, often after 11.00p.m. and lasting for two or three hours. On these nights, the plaza would overflow with locals, students and tourists alike, arriving early to find a seat at one of the al fresco cafes, which lined the plaza. One could sit and drink, eat and watch the festivities in comfort with camereros at our beck and call.

In the summer of 1996, one hit, in particular, had become a number one classic and had shot the group Ketama to fame. The song *"No Estamos Lokos"* (We're not crazy) had roared up the charts, sending dancers in nightclubs and bars into a frenzy. One hot summer night, Ketama was the main attraction. Over two days, the sound stage was erected with lights and enormous sound speakers and an eager crowd gathered at lunch time to ensure good vantage spots. There was standing room only as the enormous crowd swelled in size and drank, sang and danced together in endless revelry. The concert was a brilliant success, the voices of young and old within the plaza resounding in one enormous voice to the lyrics of that famous song.

"Semana Santa" (Holy week) was more sobering. I had arrived in Spain in April during the famous week of processions re-enacting the Passion of Christ, leading up to Easter. In Madrid, there were enormous processions through the city, each with their own sombre bands and flags and colour schemes. Priests and choirboys carried enormous statues of Mary 'Our Lady' and the crucified Christ. The streets were packed to the brim to witness these processions. The crowds formed an integral part of the drama being enacted. Many women marched barefoot, holding candles, their ankles tied with chains to symbolise the agony of Christ's march. Others whipped themselves, wore masks and white or black hoods reminiscent of both the KKK and executioners. The followers carried flaming torches, incense, banners, and flags. It was an eerie and sobering week symbolising the duality of life and death, of external salvation and damnation, the essence of the sacred Mystery and the passion of Christ. In every town or village, there was a profound, almost primeval mood during the Holy Week.

Wanting to experience the overwhelming solemnity first hand, craning my neck and standing on tiptoe, I was almost smothered by the tumultuous crowd, eager to witness the spectacle. Thousands of people choked the streets leaving me daunted by the size and gravity of the processions and the religious fervour which seemed to have so many people under its spell.

But following the solemnity of Easter's Semana Santa, Spain was again ready to party.

In the south of Spain, lies the region of Andalucía, the traditional home of flamenco and "cante jondo", the anguished lyrics, which accompany the flamenco guitars. In April, after the Easter processions the region celebrates with a mammoth six-day "feria", a carnival in Sevilla to reward itself for the piety of Lent.

Visiting the Feria had been Shami's idea and it had developed into a girl's weekend that included Jamie and Ashley. We decide to skip Friday's language classes and travel 12 hours overnight by coach to experience some of the six-day carnival. As morning broke and the sun rose, we arrived in the narrow cobbled streets of old Seville, which were ablaze with colour. Red geraniums dripped from pots on every balcony and elegant horse-drawn carriages clip-clopped between clubs and bars. Tickets to bullfights were sold from every corner and thousands of tourists strolled the streets.

The night was just as colourful with carnival lights, sideshows, amusement rides and brightly lit tents surrounding us as far as the eye could see. Food stalls, fairy floss, donuts, and the smells of other western delights merged with those of sizzling empanadas, freshly fried churros and tortillas and Sangria were consumed by the keg.

In the adjoining fields, a tent city of over one thousand pavilions stretched for two miles. This was the city of dance, from which private parties, flamenco music, and dancing spilled onto the dusty roads, twenty-four hours a day for six days. Every Spanish woman and girl, for the duration of Feria, wore the traditional flamenco costume and with arched backs and stamping feet, clicked their castanets to the live music, which never seemed to stop. As we watched the lightning-fast footwork of the experts in admiration, all inhibitions disappeared. I grabbed Shami's hand and we joined the novices dancing in the street as every joyful face raised their hands, clapped, and twirled their wrists - the women playfully flouncing their skirts and men arching their backs in happy celebration.

Not having experienced *"las corridas de toro"* (the bullfights) ever before, we bought cheap seats in the shade. On Saturday afternoon, we lined up and entered the ring with our complimentary fans whirling, laughing and chatting loudly, full of anticipation. A fanfare of trumpets heralded the start of the first of six kills for that afternoon. Around us, the crowd was swelling as the Spanish men and women, cheered and clapped the carefully padded horses, sequined matadors and pin adores, as they paraded the arena in a whirl of pomp and ceremony. But it was to be a grisly afternoon. As each successive majestic bull snorted and stamped its way closer to death, dripping with blood, each of us retreated slowly into our own private thoughts. The gallant fight to the death between man and bull, did not seem as impressive as Hemingway had painted. Shocked and saddened by the brutality and confused by the aggression showed by the crowds lusting after the death of those majestic animals, we quietly left the ring, reluctant to return. It remains for me still, one of Spain's darker barbaric sides, a blood sport which has not adapted with the changing views of most western nations.

Village street, Alberca, Spain

*Let's explore what's around
each bend, unafraid* TS

Worlds Apart

And the people of this world?
They are more varied than the stars in the
sky, and yet we are all the same. TS

"Why aren't you married?"

I laughed. If I had a dollar for every time someone asked me that question…

I looked at Rechdawi, wondering if he wanted the long or the short answer. He stared back at me patiently, then sensing my hesitation asked:

"Quieres tomar un cafe juntos?" (Would you like to have a coffee together?)

He wanted to hear the whole story. I smiled a *"sure, why not?"* smile.

A small boy appeared with two steaming glasses of sweet cafe con leche. Pulling up a small stool, Rechdawi invited me to join him. It was afternoon and the markets were crowded. Tourists were everywhere mingling at his table, admiring his jewellery imported from Morocco and roaming through the winding streets of Salamanca, enjoying the sunshine.

Only minutes before I had been enjoying my ice cream, wondering how to kill an hour or two.

TS had become my constant happy companion and I felt relaxed and carefree in her company. We would often spend hours alone together until a new friend appeared. Now I was in conversation, in Spanish with a Moroccan hippie who, before the afternoon was through, would invite me to travel throughout Spain with him by car visiting fiestas, where he would sell his jewellery.

Rechdawi was relaxed, unshaven and had that characteristic sweet smell of sweat and cologne so typical of the Arabic men of the south. His warm black eyes twinkled in his deeply tanned, handsome face as he spoke. I noticed that he possessed the most perfectly formed gentle hands and fingernails I had seen on a man. Something about his manner was soothing, quiet, and contemplative.

Born in Morocco, he had travelled extensively around Europe in his younger days enjoying the freedom and adventure of open love, relationships, hashish and pondering the meaning of life. Now in his early forties, he was still a hippie. I noticed he wore nice shoes. The stall must be doing well.

As we started to chat, I relaxed and listed to the rhythm of his speech. Caught up in the dance, my Spanish started to flow. I understood his every word, every phrase was familiar. These were the words I had learnt in the classroom. It was real. Spanish was alive and all around me.

We settled into a relaxed chat about travel, relationships, my Spanish studies, his homeland and mine, the way people have changed. He had failed to find a partner with whom he could share his life. He reminisced about his younger days when he remembered people were more open, simpatico, and honest and shared their material possessions, feelings, and thoughts. He loved to chat and loved to listen. He had friends in many countries but no real home. He was non-materialistic, a thinker and a vagabond.

"Que tipo de mujer te gusta?" I asked wondering what kind of woman he was looking for.

"Como tu" (Like you) came back the answer.

"Oh no. Not again" I thought and laughed. Was this not the crux of my ongoing dilemma? Irrespective of where I would travel in the world, the men who are most attracted to me are often Latin vagabonds, waiters, bus drivers, muy simpatico, contemplative, unmaterialistic, poor, honest, and with vastly different standards of living to mine.

These were lovely men offering what seemed like an impossible future.

Javier was one such lovely man. Tall, dark and handsome, he had a kind and patient manner. He owned the Litro Bar in Salamanca, which was famous with American students for the litre glasses of beer, spirits, and sangria or wine, they could purchase cheaply. The Litro was a drinking hole to fill up and become merry before moving on to dance bars and clubs. It was a small, dark bar, packed with dozens of young grunge Americans unable to hold their beer. Loud music and happy drunken crowds, spilled onto the street.

During our first visit to the bar one evening, Shami had approached me. We had bought drinks and were standing outside in the street where it was cooler.

"The bartender wants to meet you," she said with a wicked smile.

"Pardon. Who?" I asked.

"The cute guy behind the bar. Dark hair, fabulous eyes. He asked me who you were and wants to meet you"

I looked through the windows, my curiosity aroused. I could definitely see some potential there. Javier could speak no English and I struggled to understand him above the noise. However, before the night was through, he had offered to take me on a day trip in the country. The next day, taking Shami, Jami, and Ashley with me for protection, the five of us took off in his car and spent a superb day exploring the little Spanish pueblo of Alberca and picnicking in the countryside. The girls gave me silent, raised eyebrows and thumbs up. He was charming and intriguing, had passed the safety test and now I was keen to get to know him better.

In the weeks that followed, Javier, I realised, was a wonderful Spanish teacher. In the few spare hours of his day, we would meet. Patient and interested in Australia, we spent stolen hours chatting, eating, drinking and dancing.

He was tall with a smooth olive complexion, blue eyes, and dark curly hair. He had a scent of smoke and alcohol which I found surprisingly relaxing in a comforting way. His white shirt sleeves were always rolled up exposing his tanned and strong forearms. His hands were confident from a life pouring drinks behind the bar and commanding control of nightly revelry and yet I sensed a gentle spirit. As we joined the hundreds of couples, walking hand in hand and kissing in the sunshine, I felt my chameleon returning. Spaniards, I had discovered, with all their energy and love of life, have no inhibitions about expressing their feelings. They are a fiery, passionate people who love to love no matter where they are. It is a wonderful characteristic that I was enjoying immensely.

"Where is all this going?" I asked myself.

"Oh be quiet! It doesn't matter. Just enjoy today while you can," TS whispered.

Ok then!

How I loved my two worlds - my middle-class corporate lifestyle and my alternative bohemian cafe life, filled with long hours discussing travel, religions, politics, and philosophy with deep honest people such as him. Those wonderful Latin men who filled my vacations with wonder, warmth, affection and so much 'simpatico', remain today, warm lasting memories that I will always cherish.

Coll Baix Playa, Mallorca

Sunshine, girlfriends and Margaritas. Signoritas this is paradise! TS

Mallorca – Isle of the beautiful

Now more than ever do I realize that I will never be content with a sedentary life. I will always be haunted by thoughts of a sun-drenched elsewhere.

Isabelle Eberhardt: Swiss Explorer, Author: *"The Nomad"*

Final exams were nearly over and it was time to hit the coast. I longed to escape the flat dry pastoral interior of the Castilla and Leon region of Spain that had been my home and see the Mediterranean. Fantasies of lazy days on the beach, working on my tan, drinking cool cocktails by a pool filled my mind. The excited buzz of travel plans echoed daily outside the Courses Internationales classrooms. The excitement was building as students prepared for a month of travel before heading back to their home countries. The coast was definitely the place to be.

"Hi, I don't know you but are you interested in coming to Mallorca? I've found a really cheap package deal. I need two more people but we have to go next week before the prices go up."

Her name was Anna-Maria and she was from Norfolk, Virginia, USA. In a typical American, no holds barred approach, she smiled openly and added teasingly,

"It's a great deal, you'll love it!"

It only took about thirty seconds to say *"Sure! Great idea."*

Mallorca is part of the Baleares Islands off the eastern coast of Spain. Located smack in the Mediterranean, they attract 1.7 million European tourists each year and are considered to be a land where the rich and famous play. Jagged limestone peaks and cliffs of the Sierra de Tramontana plunge down along the Northwest coast of Mallorca. Yet on every other shore, secluded half-moon aquamarine bays with dazzling white sand seductively lure sun seekers.

From our hotel balcony in downtown Palma, the island's capital, we could see at least two km of beach and just a small portion of the five hundred kilometer coastline. Below us, beautiful people basked around the pool in the afternoon sun. It was going to be the perfect week.

Anna-Maria had an Italian mother and she spoke fluent French and Italian. A language teacher in America, she had no knowledge of Spanish when she had arrived in Spain, yet within three months she had become fluent to the point of receiving compliments from local people.

"I've studied my ass off this summer, man!" she often exclaimed. Her Italian and French background had made it easier for her to quickly pick up the language but she was also a dedicated student with a keen desire to learn.

She was short and pretty, with long straight dark hair and a gutsy, fun positive personality, which seemed to hold no inhibitions. She liked to party and she liked to shop. Single, and thirty-five years of age, she and I were two of the oldest language students at the university and we bonded instantly.

"Are you in a relationship at home?" she had asked me one day.

"No" I laughed. *"I'm avoiding dysfunctional ones!"*

"Oh man, we have to talk!" she exclaimed and laughed loudly.

The rest of the afternoon was spent in a tiny wooden Spanish bar drinking wine and exchanging very funny and some sad true-life accounts.

By the time the afternoon was over, we drunkenly toasted our resilience to the roller coaster of love each of us had experienced. Spain, for both of us, was a time of breaking free, of therapeutic carefree days and uninhibited spontaneity to do as we liked.

"You two just go and bond and don't worry about me" Johanna had teased. *"I haven't had any juicy broken romances or heartbreaks about life yet."*

It was true. At twenty-three, Johanna spoke fluent Japanese and had just finished a year's stay in Japan. She was still not quite ready to settle into a nine to five routine and had decided to try Spanish for the summer and then head to England to find work. She was an Australian, very fair with straight thin blond hair and difficult skin, which caused her some grief. Like so many Australians, she was a solo traveller, very independent and courageous but also surprisingly vulnerable and innocent at times.

When Anna Maria and I laughed and talked openly about sex and men, Johanna would listen sometimes, surprised and thoughtful. Yet she was the most relaxed, easy going woman I had met and I admired her serenity and quietly amused smiles.

The temperature had reached thirty-eight degrees. We had spent three days, plunging into the crystal green-blue waters of the pool, basking amidst the throngs of German, French and English tourists. During warm evenings we would saunter along the boardwalks, eating ice cream and watching the sunset. At night, the promenades would burst into colour with buskers and stalls selling trinkets and souvenirs.

One evening I watched in awe as a young professional spray paint artist, quickly and expertly, created vivid science fiction moonscape posters. Kneeling on the sidewalk over meters of newspaper and wearing a breathing mask, he would pull various spray paints from his kit and within ten minutes create posters of new worlds, aliens, spaceships landing on deserted moons backed by vibrant suns. Then, sealing the paint, he would spray it with a mysterious substance and set it alight for a split second in a burst of flame. Someone would instantly buy a painting in the large crowd, which had gathered around his electric light.

Restaurants spilled onto sidewalks, and car hires and tour operators called amicably in Spanish and English to passers-by. It was a shopper's paradise. Expensive leather handbags sold for a song and "T" shirts and leather shoes were sold by the dozens. We sat on the sea wall and talked for hours, watching the parade of passers-by, enjoying the warm balmy nights and marvelling at the sheer pleasure of just being there, in the moment, under a million stars near the sea.

But it was a big island and we wanted to explore every inch of it. Unlike the British colonies, the Spanish drive on the right, which offered an interesting variation on my style. With windscreen wipers mistakenly thrashing every five minutes as I struggled to remember the location of the indicators and gears, we kangaroo hoped our way out of the resort and onto the highway.

We headed out of Palma and meandered west along the coast, discovering each little resort filled cove with its variety of up-market shops and restaurants. But we became rapidly aware of our apparent poverty. We were surrounded by scantily clad Europeans, who were toasted brown and sported impeccably white teeth and designer sunglasses. Women with hourglass figures and designer clothes casually shopped for groceries in gold lama sandals. Retired couples with apparent millions in disposable income wondered casually along the boardwalks sporting gold jewellery. White was the colour of the day. White sets off the tan and co-ordinates well with the white washed million dollar apartments. Brown legs, meters high seemed to grow out of the short skirts of the German women, much to the enjoyment of their male partners.

The three of us lowered our sunglasses as we scanned the scenes with raised eyebrows. Looking down at our student sneakers we couldn't help but laugh. We hadn't brought our designer collections with us! Seduced by these little coves, we would stop the car and go for quick dips, amused by the "g" string bikini-clad middle-aged Germans who were so unashamedly brazen about their bodies. Johanna and Anna Marie, both fair and conscious of the intensity of the sun, covered up. In their one-piece bathing suits, sarongs and large shady hats and sunglasses, they proudly posed for hilarious photos next to unsuspecting near naked Germans, fast asleep, cooking slowly on the sand.

Back on the road, crossing the Sierra Tramontana, we drove north to Puerto de Soller high on the East coast and followed the train tracks down into the beautiful bay of Soller. Beautiful and scenic citrus groves and pine covered mountains rose through the mist. A warm and humid soft rain began to fall as Anna deftly squeezed our four cylinder car between two ostentatious BMW's vacationing on the glistening side street.

Our hopes of walking the thirty minutes to the beach were dampened by the weather and we wondered inquisitively around the port, stopping for the obligatory freshly squeezed orange juice. Dozens of white luxury yachts bobbed contentedly in the harbour. It was a peaceful place in the rain, tropical and casual with only a hidden scent of classy money. But as we headed to the northern gulf, the rain increased, lashing at the windows and wind whipped the palm trees. The temperature dropped and grey clouds hung over the mountains. It was warm in the car. The thunder roared ominously and through the fog, I could see scantily clad tourists running to their cars.

The northern coast of Mallorca is rugged and more exposed to the Mediterranean than the east. We decided to take the coast road and go past the tourist port of Pollencia to the isolated lighthouse outpost of Cabo Formentar. Hugging the narrow highways, we swept round each breathtaking bend marvelling at the crashing waves. When a minibus of Italian tourists parked next to us on a particularly exposed lookout, Anna couldn't help but make conversation. Soon, animated laughter and exchanges of family history, Italian camaraderie and food had warmed both the vehicles.

"I can't eat another thing and I'm sure I have put on at least two kilos!"

It was the truth. We were back in the warmth of the sun at our resort after a day of caves, more beaches and tourist towns of the east coast. Our final smorgasbord had been eagerly devoured. Soon we would find ourselves in Spanish-speaking Madrid, surrounded by the true sights and sounds of Spain, which had been so lacking in Mallorca's paradise. From there, we would all head out our separate ways.

Rouges and bullies are all part of the adventure. You can handle anything if you apply what you have learned. TS

Robbed

*You have untapped strength inside that
emerges when life tests you.
Find it. TS*

The train lurched violently as it braked to enter the underground metro station. I found myself swinging precariously, my wrist caught in the overhead strap, which thankfully had broken my fall. The train from central Madrid to Chamartin was packed with locals and tourists travelling to strange and wonderful destinations.

"Perdona, perdona."

The young man smiled as he too recovered his balance and helped me regain my feet. He was behind me and smiling. Suddenly he began to dust me down. I remembered stories of men working in pairs, spraying mustard or sauce on unsuspecting tourists from behind to distract them while they were robbed. My suspicions were aroused.

"What are you doing?"

I was worried and looked over my shoulder anxiously.

"No te preocupes" he said, grinning mischievously as he quickly excused himself, and with a laugh lurched out of the train with his friend as the automatic doors opened. They were lost in the throng in seconds.

Confused, I looked around and down to see with dismay that my daypack was wide open against my body and my wallet was gone.

Rage erupted inside me, in that one moment as I saw the automatic doors snap shut in front of me. Spanish women clutched their bags to themselves and looked the other way. Over a dozen people must have witnessed my plight and they did nothing. Seconds were ticking by as the train silently left the station and rolled into the blackness of the tunnel. My mind raced. What was in my wallet? I racked my brains to remember. I had just withdrawn AUS$250 cash for my trip north. My visa card, student card and yes there had been my AUS$40 train ticket from Chamartin to Oviedo. My heart sank. TS shook her head in amazement at my naiveté.

I just couldn't believe myself! How could I have been so foolish to fall for that trap? Thankfully my passport, airline tickets, and visa details were close to my body in my security pouch. What a bloody idiot I had been. I should have seen it coming. I continued to angrily reprimand myself for the next few minutes before snapping out of it. I sensed TS raise her eyebrows and look at me assertively. *"It is what it is Jules. Deal with it"*.

What was I going to do? I only had half an hour at Chamartin before my six hour train journey to Oviedo in the north of Spain, where my friends were due to pick me up. Above all, I wanted to cancel my visa card, but first I had to withdraw money and buy a new train ticket.

At Chamartin, the bank queue was twelve people deep, the ticket counter was worse and the clock was ticking. My blood pressure was rising by the second and I was paranoid about keeping both eyes on my luggage. Oh, the challenges TS brings! Finally, after withdrawing my money, I had only five minutes to spare. In desperation I decide to jump the ticket queue. Dragging my luggage behind me and with real American 'attitude,' I approached the counter and loudly pleaded my case in the best and fastest Spanish I could muster, demanding a ticket instantly. Either the clerk was totally afraid of the madwoman in front of him or he genuinely understood what I said, would never be known. Without a word he handed over a ticket much to the annoyance of the customers I had brushed aside.

I raced for the train with my visa card still active. Nearly two hours had now passed. I groaned as I found my seat and collapsed for the next six hours. My bank balance would be empty by the time I reached Oviedo. I would have to return home to Australia a pauper, defeated and very pissed off. My stomach was in knots.

In desperation, I sought the train conductor with the hope that I might be able to make a call from a station along the way. Speaking as slowly and as clearly as I could in Spanish, I explained my situation to him. To my absolute joy, he actually seemed to understand my plight. Yes, he said the call could be made, but *he* would have to do it from the next station, as passengers were not allowed to leave the train. If I could give him my details, he would cancel the card for me as soon as we reached the next stop. In haste, I enthusiastically gave him all the details of my card and the phone number of Visa International and thanked him for his assistance, then returned to my seat. It was only then that I realised what I had done. Now I had two good reasons to look forward to an empty bank account. What if I never saw the conductor again? My Spanish was not good enough to argue with him if he denied the conversation with me. With all my Visa details, he could bleed me dry. I slumped in my seat in despair and stared out the window oblivious that the scenery had begun to change.

Unlike the hot, flat plains of the Castilla y Leon region, the north coast of Spain is rugged and rocky with the magnificent towering peaks of the Cordillera Cantabrica, famous for its hunting, fishing, bush walking and prehistoric art. The north coastal region is divided into two principal regions, Asturias with its capital Oviedo, and Cantabria, with its capital Santander.

I was headed to Oviedo to visit my Spanish tutor Belem who had taught me Spanish in Australia but had returned to her home in the northern province. Belem's husband Jose used to lecture at Flinders University in Adelaide and I had met Belem through the Vocational Language Learning Centre where I had undertaken an intensive ten-week course in Spanish. Belem had been a wonderful tutor and she had spent many hours with me, one-on-one taking me through my paces.

After an hour and a half, we chugged into the first of many stations. I waited and waited expectantly. Five minutes passed, then ten and slowly the train moved out of the station. I craned my neck, waiting expectantly for the train conductor to return to the carriage and tell me all was OK. The train chugged on. But no one came.

I stood, feeling ill and over the tops of the seats, I scanned the faces of passengers. Desperately in a loud voice, I asked if anyone in the carriage could speak English. Heads shook and people glanced away. I sat down feeling stranded and alone, wanting to share my predicament with an English speaking person. The gentleman opposite me had been politely ignoring my depression but soon he found it difficult to contain his silence.

"Perdona, senora" he said. *"Tengo una amiga...habla ingles."*

His friend in the next carriage was a Spanish woman who spoke perfect English. With a smile, he went in search of her and returned, leading a beautiful woman with a concerned but reassuring smile.

"Do you need some help?" she inquired.

I felt myself grin with relief from ear to ear. At last, here was someone who could understand me. Doña Maria was kind and before long had made my problem her own.

"It is terrible that such a thing should happen to you in our country" she sighed. *"Unfortunately here in Spain we have many boys who do these things, but we can fix this for you"*.

She left the carriage in search of the train conductor and returned with him ten minutes later. Together we asked him about the Visa details. The conductor spent some time speaking quickly in Spanish to Doña Maria who listened to him intently. The story seemed complicated but soon she turned to me and smiled.

"Senor Martinez had telephoned Visa International when the train stopped. He had some difficulty getting through but yes, he has given them

your details and requested that your card be cancelled. The Visa people would not cancel the card without your authorisation; however, they will put an international freeze on use of the card until you telephone them on this number and confirm that the cancellation should proceed. You must telephone within the next eight hours."

I felt my legs go weak with relief. The chances of losing all my savings were considerably reduced. I spontaneously hugged Doña Maria and vigorously shook hands with Senor Martinez, over-run with gratitude for their assistance. There were smiles all around. Doña Maria and her friend Don Jorge invited me to join them in the club car for a drink where they summoned the cameraro and we spent the rest of the afternoon drinking red wine. Before long, Senor Martinez also joined us for a quiet drink as he passed by on his rounds. My spirits were uplifted. The world was full of wonderful people. Once again, when I was least expecting it, help was always close at hand. I felt 'watched over', truly blessed and simply could not stop smiling. I suddenly looked out the window and realised that the landscape had changed from brown plains to rugged green hills.

By the time the train chugged into Oviedo, I felt very relaxed and was eager to finalise the cancellation of my card. The call took only a few minutes and a new card was promised to me within twenty-four hours, delivered to my door. The ordeal over, I was ready for the adventures ahead.

I sensed the energy of TS all around me. She was chuckling.

Pouring the sidra in Covadonga, Austurias

Let's pour it, scull it,
savour it
as it spills deliciously
down our necks! TS

Austurias

*Traveling solo does not always mean you're
alone. Most often, you meet marvellous people
along the way and make connections
that last a lifetime.*

Jacqueline Boone: American Writer: *"6 Months to Live"*

The decaying grey mining and steel town of Oviedo in northern Spain is the industrial purgatory that one must endure to traverse the rugged green mountains and valleys of Asturias' beautiful "Picos de Europa", the famous national park that I planned to visit. Belem's smiling face was a bright spark in the dull station. She and her husband Jose welcomed me warmly and whisked me off to their city apartment to meet their teenage children, Coba and Carlos. I wanted to relax for a few days, with them before exploring the north.

Belem, my Australian-Spanish teacher, and mentor, with her slim forty something figure and blond bobbed, hair, is a warm and inviting woman. Jose is dark and confident with an unruly mop of black hair and thick black moustache, glasses and a piercing intensity. Their son Carlos shares his father's dark good looks. Coba, their daughter was a slim teenage girl with straight brown long hair and puppy eyes.

I was looking forward to impressing Belem with my Spanish and she was more than complimentary, I suspect exceedingly so. I am sure my grammar left a lot to be desired and it wasn't long before my el Espanol Basico paled into insignificance as I listened to their family chatter. Although I was translating much faster, the concentration exhausted me. I knew they could all speak English very well and I yearned to speak it with them so that I could relax. But to their credit, they wouldn't hear of it!

It was in the early hours of the morning that the nauseousness began. By dawn, I had a splitting headache and was throwing up at regular intervals. My head was spinning and I was unable to stand. Belem called a doctor and I was diagnosed as suffering delayed stress from the excitement of the day before. Oh! How I wished I could die from embarrassment. Nothing could settle my stomach and twenty-four hours passed before I could eat.

For the next four days, I must have been a very tiresome guest. The food of Asturias is far spicier than the food of the Castilla y Leon region and I was paranoid that my pathetic stomach would suffer a relapse.

In addition, I had to report my stolen wallet to the police for insurance purposes and fill out numerous forms. My Spanish visa was also due to expire and the police in Madrid had told me to apply for an extension when I reached Oviedo. Belem and Jose went out of their way to use their contacts to get an extension for me, a process that seemed incredibly tied up in red tape and unnecessary paperwork. There was lots of waiting around and endless documentation. The process required many trips to the police station.

Embarrassed by all the trouble I had caused them, I was ready to leave when Belem invited me to join them for a few days at their holiday house on the coast. Although I love TS, there is nothing quite like being wrapped in cotton wool by a family who genuinely cares about your welfare. I was touched. I had caused them enough trouble already and it was time to show my appreciation. I vowed to be as helpful as possible in gratitude for their hospitality.

Asturias is beautiful. Even in summer, it is rugged and rocky and cool, shrouded in mist and rain, a world away from the beaches of Majorca. Plunging gorges and cold lonely coastlines, desolate beaches and winding mountain roads are part of the everyday scenery. Our drive took us four hours northeast to a tiny coastal village. It was wild and windswept, romantic and isolated. Narrow, one car winding lanes lined with high stone walls meandered throughout the countryside. Tiny old men and women shuffled down lanes to tiny thatched shops. Locals stopped and chatted to each other over stone walls and watched as we slowly drove by.

Belem and Jose's holiday home was literally a hundred-year-old dilapidated stone farmhouse when they had bought it. Over two summers, the family had restored the two-story property, transforming it from a damp pile of rubble to a warm and cosy country home. Low ceilings were supported by dark and heavy wooden beams. Old-fashioned slightly imperfect glass filled the small downstairs lounge room windows. Large bright rugs covered the cobbled stone floors and comfortable country furniture welcomed the traveller to stop and rest. A steep wooden staircase led to the upstairs bedrooms with low hanging pitched ceilings and tiny wood framed shuttered windows. Belem had painted the bedrooms blue and had bought cast iron beds, colourful rugs with matching dunas and curtains. The interiors were like the rich culture of the country. From my bed, the view was magnificent. I could see the Gulf of Biscay. I let out a sigh of contentment. A true country getaway.

Jose busied himself and set to work restoring the original garden wall with stone and mortar. Corba, and Carlos often disappeared to the local towns where they re-aquatinted themselves with their friends from the last summer. Belem and I would go on endless walks for hours in the countryside, stop at the tiny village shops and chat to the locals. In the afternoon, she'd cook chorizo (spicy sausages), fabes (beans), soups and 'fabada' with 'mortiga' (beans with black sausage), a speciality of the region. Family friends would drop in and exclaim in wonder at Jose's more recent restorations. As it was customary for the guests to stay for dinner, local wine and guitars would be brought out, the fire lit and the evening spent singing Spanish songs at the top of their voices. My knowledge of sing-a-long Spanish tunes was restricted to well-known classics such as 'Guantanamera", "Ojos Españoles" (Blue Spanish Eyes), 'Viva España and 'Amigos Para Siempre' (Friends for Life) from the Barcelona Olympics. Hours past, rugged in the warmth of family life.

Some visitors would stay the night. On one of these occasions, Jose declared a day off work and took us on a day excursion to the borders of the mountainous Pico de Europa National Park. The town of Cangas de Onis was the original capital of Austurias, a colourful, picture postcard setting, nestled in the mountains. From there, the winding mountain roads stretch up, up into the mists and snowy peaks of the Picos to Lakes Enol and Ercina. Even in summer, the winds were bitingly cold as they raced across the open rocky moors.

Warm in the car, we headed for the tiny mountain town of Covadonga, famous for its pale pink neo-gothic basilica that rises high above the town. The Santa Cueva (Holy Cave), or grotto, deep in the mountainside, also draws tourists from all over the world that come to pray to the Virgin Mary.

By late afternoon, however, we had settled into a small bar eating local tapas and drinking 'sidra', (local bitter apple cider) which is traditionally poured from a bottle held high, into a glass in the other hand, about three feet away. The force from the cider hitting the glass releases the sidra's bouquet. Barmen aim to make the pouring quite a spectacle and manage to do it without spilling a drop unlike my hilarious attempt, which resulted in only a small sip being captured at the bottom of the glass. With evening, the stillness and freshness of the mountains dripped with solitude. It was a long, quiet drive home. Through the misty car windows, the world seemed an endless, spiritual place offering unlimited beauty and friendships to be cherished.

Quit the 'poor me' self-talk!
Be the heroine in
your own story. TS

Ill and Alone

To travel is worth any cost
or sacrifice

Elizabeth Gilbert: American Author: *"Eat, Pray, Love"*

I had packed and re-packed and taken out every unnecessary piece that I could manage and still survive comfortably in rain, cold, and sun for the next three weeks – all in just one small backpack. Belem and Jose had offered to look after my extra things.

Even with the tenacity, confidence, and humour that I had learnt from TS, there is still a vulnerability I feel prior to any solo journey, questioning if I have what it takes to cope with what life will throw at me. I had always been one for thorough planning and getting on with the job. To go boldly forth alone with only a sketch has always been a bitter-sweet concoction of anticipation and wonder, particularly in a non-English speaking country.

However, TS was always by my side, this was an adventure and I knew that I was bigger on the inside than I had allowed myself to believe. Armed with that thought, I was excited to explore the rest of Asturias and Cantabria and travel through their lofty deep green mountains and towering peaks. I wanted to talk to people in Pais Vasco, the Basque region that was fighting for independence. I wanted to visit San Sebastian, and Pamplona for the "running of the bulls" festival, and to walk in the Pyrenees.

With such a rough sketch, I set forth alone for three weeks to explore the North. After all, it was either go alone or don't see it at all and as Eleanor Roosevelt had said, *"You must do the things you think you cannot do."*. TS concurred and pointed at my chest.

Aware of an annoying cough and slight sniffle that had started bothering me two days before, I asked Belem to stop at the village pharmacy to buy cough mixture and Ventolin before my train and bus journeys, and just as well. Twelve hours later, as my bus pulled into Santander on the north coast, I was snivelling and red-eyed, with a rasping cough that smoker's boast of. With a pounding head, a fever and a bag full of used soggy tissues, I headed to the information counter with my Visa card.

'Por favor, estoy muy muy enfermo y necesito una habitación muy bueno --cuatro estrellas. Puede ayudarme?'

I was sick and my body was exhausted. I wanted a four-star hotel for the night. I was in no mood for roughing it.

Handing over my Visa card, the Rex hotel welcomed me with a red carpet. The desk clerk took pity on me, carried my bags to my room and brought me aspirin. As I walked into the spotlessly clean, warm and palatial room, I knew that I had made the right decision. Before long, I was showered, drugged and safely wrapped between the clean white sheets of a gigantic bed, comatose.

Unfortunately, travelling on a budget does not allow for palatial rooms. After two nights I had to move hotels and I spent the following three days camped in a single attic room in the Hostel Real in Santander taking drugs, coughing my lungs inside out, sucking Ventolin and cradling a high fever.

TS was a bitch. While I yearned for room service she sent me out to shop for food, water, and tissues. When I lay crying on the bed, she threw me my Swish army pocket knife and watched silently as I painstakingly made cheese and tomato baguettes for breakfast, lunch, and dinner. We argued over plans. I wanted to go home. She told me I was pathetic. I wanted to go back to the Rex hotel. She said I was soft and reminded me that I had asked to be tested.

"Not like this!" I stammered.

"Humph!" she snorted.

It was much later that month, that I realized that I had contracted bronchitis and it would be weeks before my health improved and antibiotics ended my bad dream. TS just smiled knowingly and said *"See!! I knew you'd pull through".*

"Thanks girlfriend".

The coastline during that time was a drug-induced blur. I passed through many towns, a day here, and a day there - Laredo, Urdiales, Bilbao and Zumaia came and went - a confusion of sights, kind faces, and cheap food. When I was able, I hired a taxi to drive me around the towns to show me the sights. My energy was pitifully low and I slept a lot. TS softened a bit. She found taxis for me, helped me locate shops whenever I needed them and stopped hassling me.

"Take it easy girlfriend" she whispered as I dozed on buses and in small hotel rooms. She was the best friend that I needed at those times. She stayed close, reminded me to lock my door and watched over me.

Days later, on a hot summer morning, I arrived in San Sebastian. The mountains and rain of north-eastern Spain were behind me. The temperature was thirty degrees, the sky was a deep blue and sparse cotton wool clouds floated on high. As I stood with my luggage overlooking the beautiful harbour to the Isle de Santa Clara, I instantly fell in love.

Hemingway, in "The Sun Also Rises", said that *'even on a hot day San Sebastian has a certain early morning quality. The trees seem as though their leaves were never quite dry. The streets feel as though they had just been sprinkled.'* The boulevards are wide, the buildings are stately and the parks and gardens are full of flowers. The city has been described as a 'come-here-to-die' setting, but it is not the city but the harbour and the parte vieja (old town) that enticed me and took my breath away.

San Sebastian fans around a beautiful bay that is guarded by the Isle de Santa Clara, shielding it from the Atlantic. The island could have been Enid Blyton's inspiration for the Famous Five's Kieran Island, so picturesque and well placed. The peaceful azure waters of the bay, lap onto two magnificent broad white sandy beaches of the Playa de Ondearreta and the Playa de la Concha that reach around to two headlands. On the right is Monte Urgull, a national park with gravel paths, and woods where lovers roam hand in hand. On the left is Monte Igueldo, which boasts an amusement park at its summit with views that stretch to heaven.

I stood there, statue like for fifteen minutes before I could muster enough resolve to pry myself away from the view and start the search for accommodation. San Sebastian is not a budget city. After phoning a number of hotels in my guidebook, I found a lovely, small, central hotel near the bay and settled into my single room. I was desperately tired and I knew I would have to pace myself and take it easy for a few more days. I lay down and promptly fell asleep. When I awoke it was late afternoon. I showered, changed and went out to explore. Automatically, my feet led me back to the peace of the bay. It was a healing place where I would spend each of my evenings over the next week.

By 7:00p.m. the sky was still deep blue. I sat content with TS on the sea wall and watched the water. Around me the beach was packed, toe to toe with brown bodies sprawled on colourful towels, with bare female breasts, brown masculine chests, and big bellies and trim torsos. They were there in all shapes and sizes, sun lovers frolicking in the crystal green waters of the Bay of Bahia. Teenage boys and girls, their firm young bodies tanned and healthy, paraded in groups along the shore, admiring each other, whispering and giggling behind their hands. Young children screamed in delight, playing at the water's edge, their skin glowing golden brown on that sunny beach day.

As the sun set behind the Isle de Santa Clara, San Sebastian took on an ethereal aura. Bathers began to pack up. Tired parents dragged their reluctant children behind them up the sand and slowly the beach began to empty. Peace settled over the bay. The island itself became floodlit and backlit by a full yellow moon that cast a gossamer light over the water. Dozens and dozens of yachts, moored in the lee of the island, bobbed contentedly and laughter, foreign tongues, and music could be heard all around me. Along the foreshore, soft light glowed from tall old-fashioned streetlights lining the wide seaside boardwalk and tourists and locals sauntered romantically, watching the sunset.

Over the next few days as my health recovered, I immersed myself in the beauty of the old town and beaches, returning each evening to the boardwalk where buskers played. My favourite, a classical trio always drew a crowd. Their soft mournful strains of Pachelbel's 'Canon' floated on the breeze as the three male music students mesmerized the crowd. Their cello, violin, and flute drowned me in their romantic melodies. The sun set and my heart soared with peace. Despite my illness, I cherished TS. With her, I was totally present in each moment, aware of every sound, smell, and scene, fully immersed into every day to feel it, reflect, write and just be.

To this day, every time I hear it played, Pachelbel's 'Canon' transports me back to the dusk of those warm summer evenings overlooking the gossamer water and golden sky of San Sebastian. It was a place that I returned to night after night to hear the sweet healing strains from that student trio who could move the earth and connect me to heaven.

Running of the Bulls in
Pamplona, Spain

*How much risk one
takes cannot be judged
by another for who
knows their true
heart's desire?* TS

The Running of the Bulls

Wisdom is sensing the Bull and avoiding his shit. TS

'La Fiesta Los San Fermines' has been described by Hemmingway "*as an undiluted and gripping an expression of lunacy and joy as ever careered down a city's streets.*" The 'running of the bulls' is the annual fiesta in Pamplona, made famous by Ernest Hemmingway's novel 'The Sun Also Rises'.

One hour away in San Sebastian it was quiet, warm and humid. It was a sort of day when time stands still and the sky meets the sea in a silent, calm, foggy haze and heat hangs in the air. I was on the brink of recovering from my chest infection and head cold. Looking out across Bahia Bay from the summit of Monte Igueldo, I heard my lungs wheeze. My chest felt tight. Far below, million dollar yachts breathed quietly on their moorings awaiting their owner's next excursion. The Atlantic horizon stretched for miles and disappeared quietly into the sky. The view was well worth the climb. My two American companions were exhausted.

"*Don't take anything*" they said. "*Only three days left man. Just go drink and dance and hang out. Find the Toro in you!! We didn't sleep for 3 nights in Pamplona. Our bus just got in this morning and tonight we're on the train to Barcelona. We've got to crash man, right here.*"

They passed out, and I left them snoring. The thought of Pamplona loomed before me. Could my health stand it? I was eager to find out. Hmmm.

"Can I help you?" I asked a tall, kind English man who was struggling with his Spanish at reception. My hotel room was next to the reception area and I could hear an Englishman trying to communicate with the receptionist. He turned around surprised and relieved and smiled. I liked him instantly. Together we finished his negotiations and started to chat. Ian was from Exeter and was traveling in Spain to practice his Spanish. He was a tall, blond, easy going English guy of thirty-two looking for spontaneity and adventure. He too, was keen to head south and within fifteen minutes, with images of Hemmingway's novel dancing in my mind, we agreed to travel together for a few days.

• • • • • • • ● ● ● • • • • • • • •

"You're wrong," he said. *"The imperative conjugation of the verb ends in 'e' not 'a'."* I looked at him calmly. We both thought we were right. It was a very hot beautiful summer's afternoon in Pamplona and our clothes were damp with perspiration.

"It's no use arguing," I said. *"We can look it up in the textbook later but let's just get the camerero's attention!"*

We had been waiting fifteen minutes to order drinks and a *'menu del dia'* for lunch, but the al fresco cafe was packed to the brim and there was a noticeable shortage of waiters. We were still debating on how being assertive in Spanish demands a slightly different emphasis and conjugation of the verb. In desperation to get some service, I leaned over and caught the camerero's green apron as he sailed rapidly past the table. I took the opposite tack. *"Oiga, por favor, ayudarme!"* (Excuse me - please help me?) I sighed, allowing my inner femininity to flow. It worked. He smiled, delivered his tray of drinks and returned immediately. *"Olay!"* I whispered, smiling mischievously at Ian.

We had arrived a few hours before in Irunea, Pamplona, in the region of Navarra to a cacophony of music, shouts, laughter and chaos. The streets were bursting with colourful crowds awash with wine and sangria for the annual running of the bulls. I was glad of Ian's company as we pushed headlong through each street in search of our hostel. Now as we relaxed into the madness around us, we were anticipating the evening's festivities and next morning's bull-run. The fiesta draws over one million people from all the corners of the world to party, to run, to watch and to enjoy the madness.

At the next table, a middle-aged, unshaved, retired runner with thick salt and pepper hair was animatedly explaining the proceedings to the two tourists at his table. Fascinated, we asked if we could listen and turned our chairs towards their table to join them.

Through Senor Marcelo's weathered deeply lined face, thick accent, and sangria induced happiness we were quickly drawn into a historical account of the spectacle that was to unfold again in the morning.

The fiesta, which is celebrated from the 6th to 14th July each year is in honour of San Fermin, patron saint of Navarra. The fifteenth century statue of Saint Fermin had already been paraded through the old part of Pamplona with political and religious authorities making many speeches and bestowing blessings. Unfortunately, we had also missed seeing the "*Gigantes*" (enormous wood-framed and papier-mâché puppet figures managed from inside) dance, however, in the final two days there was still plenty to experience.

The Encierro, (the Running of the Bulls) is the event at the heart of the San Fermines. Senior Marcelo pulled a napkin toward him and with his pen, drew a map of the town. Historically, the easiest way to get the bulls from outside the city walls, to where they need to be, is simply to let them run through the city streets, herded by children and adults with shouts and sticks. This is believed to date back to the thirteenth century. The festival was moved from September to July for better weather and more tourists. These days the bulls run far more frantically due to the cacophony of music, shouts, and noise as the huge crowds urge them on.

Running, are two types of bulls: *el torro bravo*, Spain's brave, fighting black bulls, and the steers, *los cabestros* who have the bells around their necks. The sound of the bell keeps the herd together and moving down the street. The six fighting *el torro bravo* bulls that will take part in the evening

79

bullfight start the run accompanied by an initial group of cabestros. Two minutes after leaving the corral in Santo Domingo, the second group of bulls, which are slower and smaller than the first ones, are also let out.

Since the 1800's daredevils from around the world dash through Pamplona's streets, ahead of the bulls dressed in traditional white trousers and white t-shirts with a red bandana around their necks. They carry rolled-up newspapers to wave at the bulls and attract their attention. National and worldwide television coverage ensure that the crowds are huge and publicity occurs, particularly when a runner is hurt, which is often.

Since 1924, over a dozen people have been killed at the festival, knocked to the ground by a bull and often struck and gored by a second animal if they try to get up. Runners are, therefore, instructed to remain on the ground if they get knocked down and cover their heads with their arms. Many people are injured each year, by the animals and the crowds as they frantically run toward the bullfighting arena through the narrow streets on slippery cobblestones.

A wooden fence defines the route of the run through the streets. Part of the fence stays in place throughout the fiesta but other sections are assembled and disassembled every day. It's a huge task, particularly as the streets are overflowing with sangria infused tourists.

Senior Marcelo stabbed his thick padded forefinger at a pamphlet on the table and spat his displeasure, discounting the list of rules and behaviour not allowed:

- People under 18 years of age must not participate.
- Waiting in corners, blind spots, doorways or in entrances located along the run is prohibited.
- Leaving doors of shops or entrances to apartments open along the route is not allowed.
- Runners may not drink alcohol or take drugs.
- Carrying objects is prohibited.
- Do not wear inappropriate clothes or footwear.

- Do not incite the bulls along the route or in the bullring.
- Running backwards towards the bulls is prohibited.
- Holding or harassing the bulls is not allowed.
- Stopping or blocking the safety of other runners is prohibited.

Although, apparently many of these rules are ignored, police do their best to keep the event as safe as possible.

Lowering his voice and suddenly appearing to sober up, with an air of mystery, Senior Marcelo drew us closer to him intimating that what he was about to tell us was important. In a hoarse voice, fuelled by booze, he whispered of the private and solemn event that tourists don't usually see.

"In the morning" he wheezed, *"when the runners are walking up the slope from the corral where the bulls are waiting, they raise their rolled newspapers and chant to an image of San Fermin that is in the wall along the path. They say "A San Fermin pedimos, por ser nuestro patron, nos guie en el encierro dandonos su bendicion."* (We ask San Fermin, being our patron saint, to guide us in the bull-run and give us your blessing). *When they finish they shout "Viva San Fermin! Gora San Fermin." This chant is sung three times, first when there are five minutes to go before 8a.m., then three minutes and one minute before the gate of the corral is opened. And so it begins!"* Senior Marcelo smiled triumphantly and fell back in his chair, refilling his glass.

The retired Senior Marcelo continued to drink all afternoon, sharing stories, laughing and slapping high fives and giving bear hug kisses to the runners who passed his table. By evening, with the bands playing, fireworks going off and the streets getting wild I headed for the hotel. My head ached, my energy was gone and I was exhausted. I excused myself leaving Ian and the other travellers to party on and fortunately, I found my way safely to bed, where I fell into a comatose sleep.

The next morning dawned bright and began early. Despite Senior Marcelo's invitation to stay awake until dawn, Ian had managed to get a few hours of sleep. As we searched to find a safe vantage point, we joined the thousands of people craning over balconies, sitting in trees and on rooftops and leaning through open windows along the route.

That morning, the Encierro was due to start at the corral in Calle Santo Domingo. Runners had to start somewhere between the Plaza del Ayuntamiento (City Hall Square) and the pink slab education building in the Cuesta of Santo Domingo. They had to be in place before 7:30a.m. When the clock on the church of San Cernin struck eight, Ian and I looked at each other and grinned recalling the secret chanting ceremony Senior Marcelo had shared with us the day before. Two rockets were launched and we knew that the corral had opened and soon the bulls would be charging behind the runners for the full 825 metres, the distance between the corral and the bullring. We had been told that the run usually lasts between three and four minutes, although on that morning, with all the excitement it felt much longer.

I could feel the excitement inside me as the first runners appeared with crazed looks in their eyes, looking behind them as they ran. As they materialised, a roar of support erupted as the crowd went wild. The first runners were followed within seconds by dozens of their peers, running, falling and ducking into doorways with the bulls at their heels as they dashed across the slippery cobbled stoned streets. But oh the bulls! Those imposingly powerful black animals, each weighing around 500kg to 700kg, their heads bowed, sweat glistening, large horns ready to gorge every runner in their path. These were the bulls to be showcased and finally killed in the bullfights that night in front of sell-out crowds.

To help shield the crowd, a large number of *'pastores'* (bull "shepherds") placed themselves behind the bulls, their only protection being a long stick. Their essential role was to stop the crowd from inciting the bulls from behind and to protect the crowd if a bull turned around and run backwards. Talk about brave!

Suddenly a third rocket was fired from the bullring, signalling that all the bulls had entered the bullring.

Although we were outside, we knew that *'dobladores'*, (ex-bullfighters), their capes whirling, had taken up position in the bullring to help the runners fan out and run to the various sides of the ring to confuse the bulls and steer them towards the bull ring corral as quickly as possible.

Then there was the fourth and final rocket, which told us that all the bulls were safely in the corral and that the bull-run had officially ended for that day. For many people, however, the celebrations were only just beginning.

Having had already witnessed the gory bullfights in Seville in April, I was not at all keen to attend the bullfight that night and go through the grisly and gruesome experience again. Ian felt the same. Those six magnificent animals running toward their death had earned our respect, far more than the million-plus crowd chanting for their demise. We agreed to stay another day to soak up the atmosphere and then plan our next move.

Ordessa valley, Pyrenees

Oh the crisp mountain air, the slanting sun and the snap of the coming cold evening. Let's share our wine with strangers who could become our friends. TS

Pyrenees and Terrorists

We are not victims
of the world we see. We are victims
of the way we see the world.

Shirley MacLaine: American Actress, Solo Traveller
Author: *"Don't Fall Off the Mountain"*

"I have a compromise," I said to Ian. *"What do you think of this?"*

We were discussing our travel options for the next week. I was keen to hire a car and drive northeast to the Pyrenees to walk in the National Park but wanted to share the costs. However, Ian was keen to go to the Basque region for a week and visit friends.

Coming to agreement took only a few minutes. That was the wonderful thing about Ian. He was extremely easy-going, accepting and flexible in his approach to life, making him an excellent travelling companion. I loved the ease with which he adapted to embrace opportunities, always present to experiencing the best that each day had to offer. Each day was an adventure when we remained present to each other and what the universe offered us. TS sat quietly in the background of my heart, smiling quietly and offering a gentle nudge whenever I absentmindedly switched back to autopilot.

The final plan included hiring a car and driving out to the Pyrenees for three days and then driving to the Basque region to catch up with one of Ian's friends who knew locals who were fighting for independence in the Pais Vasco. It was a hot spot that interested us both.

Heading northeast to the Pyrenees should only have taken an hour or two on the motorway. The route was well signposted and an easy drive but all the signs were in Spanish. As a big blue sign sailed past us on the motorway, I turned to Ian.

"I know I'm supposed to be navigating but we just missed the turn-off!"

Ian just laughed and shook his head. For the next two hours, we backtracked and side tracked our way via a number of out of the way towns and third class roads. With all the guessing, we were hours behind our rough schedule but finally we saw signs to Jaca, then Torla near Parque National de Odessa.

The Spanish province of Aragon is sandwiched between the provinces of Navarra, in the western Pyrenees, and Cataluña, the eastern Pyrenees. It stretches roughly between Pamplona and Lerida, with Zaragoza in the South as its urban hub. Parque National de Odessa is located in these Aragonese Pyrenees near the French border. It is an area where goats and sheep wander freely through rugged mountains. The crumbling ancient villages allow for a peaceful, solitary, uncomplicated lifestyle. Jagged cliffs, canyons, icy cascading rivers and some of the most beautiful peaks in the country are found there. There are also miles of trails for walkers of all levels and we were keen to explore a few of them.

Our drive took us through the lowland and foothills of the western Pyrenees of Navarra, a dry and arid area, spotted with small Spanish 'pueblos'. As we neared the Aragonese Pyrenees, the roads began to serpentine upwards around dams and deep green forests. The sky was blue and the mountains loomed high above us.

The small stone village of Torla had a wide range of accommodation available. *'Albergues'* are old, unheated buildings with bunks and cold running water. The next step up on the accommodation ladder are 'casas' with hot water and wood stoves. *'Refugios'* have tiled showers, electricity, and large clean dormitories. Blankets were provided in all. I was still coughing at regular intervals and the thought of staying in a cold poky albergue was not appealing. I knew that if got a coughing fit while in bed, there was a good chance I'd knock myself unconscious on the beams' inches above the bed head. We decided on a refugio.

It was late in the day and tired hikers young and old, dressed in shorts and hiking boots and carrying daypacks and rucksacks, plodded the village's cobbled streets. As evening fell, lights came on and twinkled through rustic windows and the clouds that had been building up all afternoon opened and drowned the mountains in mist and rain.

We spent a full day exploring a small section of the Parque and chose the '*Soaso Circle*' a seven-hour hike that took us up out of the canyon to a distant lookout. It then followed the canyon rim to its end, descended into the gorge and meandered back to the refugio. It was a magnificent day striding out in the rain and mist, walking with rugged adventurous tourists from all over Spain.

We returned to our refugio covered in mud but oh so grateful for the hot showers, clean bathrooms and comfortable beds. That night, we stayed in, while the open fire spat and crackled in the hearth and shadows danced against its roughly hewn thick stone walls. We opened a few bottles of local *vino tinto* (red wine) and laughed and shared stories with other hikers conversing in the universal language of charades while the thunder roared and the rain poured down around our sanctuary. My coughing spells had subsided at last.

• • • • • • • • ● • • • • • • • • •

Three days later we headed east to the Basque country known as Pais *Vasco*. Ian's friend Jane was visiting Spanish friends in Tolosa, a small Basque town a few hours south of San Sebastian. The journey to possibly spend some time with local Basques intrigued us both.

The Basques began fighting for an independent Basque state in northern Spain and south-western France as a result of General Franco's repressive military dictatorship in 1959. The Basque language was banned, their distinctive culture suppressed and intellectuals imprisoned and tortured for their political and cultural beliefs.

Known as ETA: Euskadi ta Askatasuna (Basque Fatherland and Liberty), their revolt began as a student resistance movement, bitterly opposed to Franco's regime. Over eight hundred people had been killed and thousands injured in car bombings and shootings. Members of ETA were listed as terrorists by the USA and European Union.

Basque language, food and culture are very unique.

There are four major Spanish dialects in Spain. Castilian is the most widespread and is taught in leading universities. Galician is spoken in Galicia in the North West. Valencian, from Valencia, dominates the southeast coast, and Catalan is from Cataluña on the north coast. Although the dialects differ, Spaniards are usually able to make themselves understood. Basque, however, is so ancient a language that it predates even Latin and is said to be one of Europe's oldest languages. It is spoken exclusively by half a million people in the Pais Vasco region of the southern Pyrenees.

Other Spaniards refer to Basque as 'la lengua del diablo' (the devil's tongue) because of its ancient origins, which few Spaniards can understand. Both Ian and I were forced to use sign language, driven mute by this strange language neither of us could understand. These language differences only reinforce the cultural and political chasm between Pais Vasco and the rest of Spain.

The cuisine of the Basque region also sets the area apart.

We arranged to meet Jane, a strong and dynamic English woman, and her Spanish friend Luciana in a small bar, across the road from our hotel on the first evening of our arrival. Jane bounded into the bar smiling broadly, followed by a very attractive Spanish woman with classic olive features and long dark hair. Luciana was obviously well known by the locals as her father had fought in many battles with police over the years. She received a warm welcome from everyone. Soon free rounds of strong local wine were coming our way, accompanied by varieties of tapas.

Tapas in the Basque region are known as *'pinchos'* and it didn't take long before we were diving into a variety of dishes, including '*bocalao a la vizcaina*' (salted cod in tomato sauce), '*chipirones en su tinta,*' (baby squid in their own ink), tangy sardines and crusty bread.

The food and wine flowed endlessly throughout the next two days as Jane and Luciana shared their hospitality with us, introduced us to local men and women and the uniqueness of their culture. Just being present to hear their passion for their homeland, their fury for the disrespect shown to their culture and their people over the decades, the incarceration and silencing of those who tried to speak out against the repression and their determination to secure a safe haven for their families are universal needs that we all share. They chose to exert their demands through violence and fear as desperate attempts to be heard and retain what was left of their homeland.

Little did we know that their fight and the violence would continue for another three decades before the militants finally lay down arms, revealed all the locations of their weapon caches to the Spanish government and conceded that they had completed disarmed.

But the mountains were calling me and my three weeks were coming to an end. Ian and I exchanged contact details and promised to reunite on my return to England. For me, there was more hiking to do in northern Spain.

When travelling alone, you have to trust your gut to keep yourself out of danger. TS

Los Picos de Europa

*Trudging alone along that black road, sometimes
in the teeth of wind and rain, gave me an
exhilarating sensation of adventure.*

Simone de Beauvoir: French Feminist, Activist, Author: *"Prime of Life"*

In May 1995, the Picos De Europa became the largest national park
in Europe, extending across three Spanish regions of Asturias, Cantabria
and Castilla y Leon - a magnificent 160,500 acres. I had seen photos of
the area and was keen to trek for a few days in the national park. Several
travellers had raved about its 2,600-meter snow covered peaks, its deep
gorges, jagged rocky mountain trails and the friendliness of the people
they encountered.

Having said goodbye to Ian, TS and I re-acquainted as old friends
do, picking up exactly where we had left off. It felt good to be with her
again and to step into the unknown. I bought a bus ticket to Poncelbos,
the main village inside the national park and remained open to whatever
would come.

I arrived in Poncelbos at midday, well read with a rough idea of the
direction I wanted to go, to find a refugio for the night. The trick was
to find the right trail and arrive at one of the lodgings early enough to
secure a bed before nightfall. I decided to walk to Bulnes, a short, less
travelled steep path up to what was described as a 'microscopic roadless

village situated amongst breath-taking scenery'. The place offered very cheap overnight accommodation in Albergue de Bulnes and was well recommended.

Turning off the main path, I soon left the hordes of day-trippers behind and was sweating it out on my own, climbing higher and higher up the jagged cliff path. Soon I was swearing to myself for letting my fitness level decline to that of a swimming pool tourist. Only one and a half years earlier I had climbed to over 6,000 meters in Argentina on a major mountain trekking expedition, yet there in the Picos, I was wheezing madly!

"If you don't use it, you lose it girlfriend" TS reminded me.

Overtaking a group of young scouts, I continued up the incline to the saddle and within two hours had arrived at the ramshackle village. Old Spanish women dressed in black sat in doorways, watching the day pass. Ancient old men, their faces withered from years in the sun, led donkeys loaded with hay along narrow trodden paths. Their rich culture oozed from their faces. High above the village, the path continued through the mountain range to the Picos' most famous mountain, Naranjo de Bulnes.

Finding the faded blue sign high on a wall, I inquired whether the albergue had space for the night.

"Si, si" came the reply and a middle-aged, slovenly, unshaven man led me to the next building, through a tiny doorway into an open dormitory housing twelve double bunk beds. Strangely, all of them were empty. In peak season, I thought it a bit odd but then dismissed it. It was still only mid afternoon

"Esta llave es para ti" (This key is for you") he said.

"And I have the other"

Handing me a large key, I felt his hand stroke mine as he looked directly into my eyes, held up the other key, smiled knowingly, and then turned away.

I stopped cold. There was something dark about him, something dangerous. Eagerly awaiting other trekkers to arrive, I dragged a well-used wooden chair out into the sunshine, closed my eyes, intent to let the afternoon pass, however, hunger soon overtook me. The scouts had set up camp across the river and outside their brightly coloured tents, were cooking a late lunch. I wandered down to the outdoor cafe. To my dismay, the staple "take away" Spanish diet of chips and eggs or bocadillos once again confronted me. Hungry and annoyed, I ordered the pork bocadillo and reluctantly handed over the exorbitant pasetas. Again, I felt the stranger's hand needlessly brush mine as he handed me the plate. He was a short man, dressed in the rustic peasant's pants and shirt, but his dark eyes seemed cold and sexual. I avoided his gaze.

No one else booked in for the night. My curiosity was aroused and I decided to explore the village. Where were all the hikers that were supposed to regularly fill this Albergue? I wondered around the old stone buildings, warmed by the heat of the sun. Young children watched me playfully, screaming with delight when I returned their gaze, ducking "peek-a-boo" behind bushes and donkeys.

A little further up the hill, a bright blue sign, "Albergue de Bulnes" caught my eye. This was strange. Wasn't I staying in "Albergue de Bulnes?" In the late afternoon light, I could see hikers with colourful rucksacks resting against old stone walls. Music drifted from what appeared to be a restaurant and trekkers relaxed on outdoor rustic benches sipping beer and talking quietly. This, actually was the albergue referred to in my guidebook! But if so, where was I?

Inquiring at the office, it was apparent that there was no space at the inn. Strictly first come first served and it was now nearly 5.00p.m. All beds were taken.

"Can you recommend another albergue for the night here in Bulnes?" I

asked in Spanish to the young woman behind the counter. She looked at me directly.

"There is another here, but I tell you only for your information," she said. *"You will have to decide"*

"Would you recommend it?" I asked again. She looked directly into my eyes.

"I cannot recommend any other," she said. *"You will have to decide".*

She shook her head and then turned to carry on with her work, not wishing to discuss it any longer.

TS raised her eyebrows and gave me that knowing look. I sensed immediately what I had to do. If there was a time to trust my intuition, it was now. I remembered again the words my best friend had written on my farewell card:

"Please look after yourself first, before any journey or any other person".

The thought of being visited by that man during the night sent shivers down my spine. It wasn't worth the risk. I returned to the albergue and hurriedly packed my things. If I left now, I could be back at Poncebos by 8.00p.m. Yes, it would be difficult descending the mountain trail in the dark and finding accommodation in the town would be expensive, but it was worth the peace of mind. Returning my key at the cafe, I apologised that I couldn't stay and I wouldn't pay. As his angry abusive yells followed me down the mountain, I smiled quietly inside. I knew I had made the right decision.

It was dark and raining by the time I reached Poncebos. My boots were covered in mud and I was wet through. The skies were black and mist covered the hilltop of Bulness from where I had come but the lights of Poncebos were warm and inviting and music streamed from the restaurants and cafes. The warmth filled my soul. Tourist laughter was in the air. As I stepped out of my hot shower and crawled into a clean comfortable bed I knew the expense was well worth the peaceful night's sleep. I may have been wrong about the stranger but I was right about one thing. I knew, I would have been awake all night, listening for his footsteps in the rain outside the albergue, feeling vulnerable, knowing there would be no one to help me if I needed it in the dead of night. TS smiled at me in acknowledgment.

The next two days in the Picos were wonderful. It rained, stormed and the skies opened pouring litres of water into the raging gullies. Laughing tourists, with families and herds of children wrapped in colourful rain gear, trudged the muddy "Ruta del Cares", one of the Pico's most famous trails. The trail 11km long had been blasted out of the mountain-side, 150mts above the raging Rio Cares. The path was constructed by the government to monitor an artificial water channel that gushes alongside as it follows the curves and gullies, high above the valley floor. Sheer cliff faces and jagged mountain peaks rose from the mist and rain as the colourful brigade of happy multinational tourists braved the weather together. I enjoyed spending most of the time walking with three male students from Leon who, rugged against the rain, were happy to complete the last day of their seven day hike through those rugged mountains. I walked over thirty five kilometers in those three days and as my coach headed back to Oviedo to pick up my luggage, I felt exhausted but exhilarated. TS had once again, brought me through quite an adventure.

Empty tables in Salamanca's Plaza Mayor as the summer ends.

A life changing summer?
Pay it forward as you leave, with renewed
kindness in your heart, a joyful smile on your
face and a generous tip on the table. TS

The Summer Ends

Travelling is like flirting with life
It's like saying, 'I would stay and love you,
but I have to go; this is my station'

Lisa St. Aubin de Teran: Adventure Traveller, English Author: *"The Hacienda"*

It was quiet outside. The cool and calm night sky was clear and pinned with a million friendly stars. The empty suburban streets of Salamanca were quietly resting, awaiting the next morning. Autumn had arrived in Spain and a cool breeze swept the pavements, rustling the leaves and sending the papers flying, swirling around my shoes.

I slowly walked home in the early hours of the morning after catching up with friends for the last time. As I strode, my thoughts drifted back over the months to my first few days in Spain and all the kindness and help I had received from Tania, Sofia and Jose at Hostel Alicante in Madrid. I thought of Doña Louisa and her wonderful laugh and stolen giggling moments with Kate in our bedrooms, during those crazy student days that I had spent at Calle de San Claudio.

My mind drifted to Paquita my lovely intercambio who had taught me so much local language; to young Alfredo, now gone and my wonderful professors; Don Juan's charades in the classroom and the boys flirting with Doña Katarina. I wondered what all my student friends were doing back in their homelands of America, Europe and Asia - Shigeko, Ingrid, Lars

Juliette Robertson

and Oliver, Ashley and Jamie and Shami who had accepted and included me as we danced, drank, studied and laughed all summer long.

My eyes welled up as I thought of Belem and Jose and their incredible generosity and friendship that they showed to me when I was exploring the north. I was drawn into the memories of Ian with his quirky English smile and relaxed easy-going nature; the food and stories that Luciana had shared; the vibrant and brilliantly fluent Anna-Marie who made me laugh so easily and the quietly independent Johanna, my wonderful travelling companions.

As I turned into my street, I smiled at the thought of tall, handsome Javier serving beer at his Litro Bar surrounded by the new semester of students who had poured into Salamanca, and I remembered with love all the warmth and affection he had shared with me.

The summer had ended, and it was time to leave Spain.

I knew that I would see my American friends again as I still had many months of travel left and I had received open invitations to visit their homes in the USA. As I walked those quiet familiar streets, memories smells, and sounds of my Spanish summer filled my head. Memories of music and dancing, of wine and laughter and early morning dawns emerging from bars to drink strong hot coffee and eat churros.

Memories of wonderfully friendly Spanish men, of beautifully dressed Spanish ladies and the sexy liveliness of life. Memories of happy day trips with student friends to explore small historical towns on long hot afternoons and walking their high stone fortressed walls and cobblestone streets.

I had walked in the sunshine protected by a bright white divine light and had been met with open hearts and helping hands. I had rediscovered spontaneity and love and joy in the stories and lives of others.

TS had become a wonderful friend. I now knew how to listen to her down-to-earth advice. I was no longer jealous of her natural beauty, sensible shoes, earthy cotton clothing and wash and wear hair, for they had become part of me. I now spoke a second language and knew how to bargain in foreign markets. She had taught me how to stand up to strangers, unafraid and ask for what was right and fair and dance with wild unabashed happiness.

It was time to begin the next adventure!

Postscript

Years have passed. Many more adventures and a continuing career, marriage, and my own children have all entered my life, since that one Spanish summer that I recall with so much joy. And when life becomes somewhat tedious or people are stressed and unkind, my mind wanders back to the days that I spent in the cobblestoned magnificent Plaza Mayor of Salamanca, sitting, studying, smiling and watching old married couples drop their parcels, raise their arms and begin to spontaneously dance to the music.... just because..... in the warm sunshine, in the sunshine, in the sunshine.

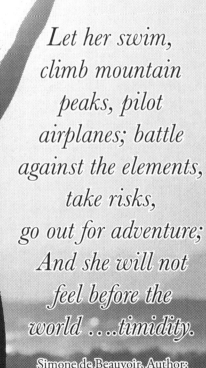

*Let her swim,
climb mountain
peaks, pilot
airplanes; battle
against the elements,
take risks,
go out for adventure;
And she will not
feel before the
world ....timidity.*

Simone de Beauvoir, Author:
"The Second Sex"

Other Stories from the Road

Juliette Robertson

*Let's face the wind
with our hair flying free
and the sun on our face.
It's time to go sailing.* TS

September Seas

I oft hear you calling, oh how I miss thee,
For you are my first love,
you are but the sea.

Kay Cottee: AO, Australian, first woman to sail solo,
unassisted around the world. Author: *"First Lady"*

I had sailed boats since I was a teenager but the yachting idea came out of the blue. We were eating pizza in a Greek cafe in Adelaide in 1990, the winter rain was dribbling down the window when someone came up with a bright idea.

"Wouldn't it be great to escape, hire a yacht and cruise the Greek islands in summer?"

We were musing dreamily at a poster of the turquoise Aegean Sea and sun-drenched, white-washed Greek villages. Six of us had our hands in the pizzas and two nearly empty bottle of red wine stood close by. We had all travelled overseas independently to interesting destinations but had never ventured to organise a trip together and although two of us knew how to sail dinghies, none of us were experienced with yachts.

"Well why don't we?" asked Paul.

"It couldn't be that hard. September in two years - on our own - the whole thing - no organised tour". Eyebrows were raised around the table.

"How long would it take to learn to sail a big, comfortable, sexy yacht?" asked Sharon.

"I know the Cruising Yacht Club and Royal SA Yacht Squadron are always looking for crew. TAFE run skippers courses. Let's look into it!"

We finished the pizza and wine with a spark ignited in our minds.

"September in two years" we called to each other as we left the cafe that evening.

"Let's do it."

Numerous dinners, letters, telephone calls and long discussions ending late into the night, followed. Within two months, three of us landed crewing positions on twelve-meter yachts at the local marinas in Adelaide. Over the next eight months, we competed in weekly day, and overnight offshore sailing races in St. Vincent's Gulf, to Kangaroo Island and Pt. Lincoln. Although the waters around South Australia can be reasonably rough and we spent quite a few nights hanging by our safety harnesses, throwing up over the side, we were hooked.

We wanted to go yachting full guns blazing and so for a year in the evenings after work, three of us attended classes at the college of Technical and Further Education. We completed our Inshore Skipper's Certificates, learning the basics about safe cruising, anchoring, radios, radar's and chart navigation.

Nearly one year after that fateful pizza, we hired a twelve meter "Beneatu First", and with a crew of six, took off across St. Vincent's Gulf to Pt. Vincent, six hours over the horizon for our first solo cruise. It was a cold but bright, perfect winter's sailing day and with a video camera rolling, we charted our course and hoisted the mainsail to a round of applause. This was, at last, the real test. By mid-afternoon, we had arrived. Locals at the Pt. Vincent Pub smiled as we toasted our success that night. Now that our first independent adventure was finally done, we couldn't wait for our epic vacation that was still one year away.

As the months passed, the logistics for the fairy tale holiday started to get more complicated, but we were inspired. We discovered that sailing the Turkish coast proved to be a more cost-effective option than Greece and seemed more interesting and mysterious. "Charter World" in Melbourne provided lots of information and advice. They booked us through Yuksel Yachting in Marmaris, Turkey. The final head count would determine the size and number of yachts needed. It was time to start putting the money on the table. Who was prepared to make the final commitment?

Of the original six, four remained plus four others had joined the group. But eight on a twelve-meter yacht did not seem very appealing. Nor did the thought of two nine meter yachts with four on each. For comfort, we wanted space. We'd need two twelve meter yachts, each comfortably accommodating six people. There seemed no shortage of volunteers. The word spread. More and more people were showing interest. *"You're going cruising in Turkey? I'd love to come and I have a friend and a son."*

I was alarmed with the number of people wanting to join in. Something told me it was time to start being really careful. The dynamics of the group were important and had to be considered carefully if we were going to happily live and party together for a few weeks. Living below deck, even on a twelve-meter yacht, can be cramped and sleeping arrangements were going to be interesting. Diplomacy was called for as some people were told that unfortunately, we had no more room. Arrangements had to be changed time and time again before the final team was agreed. When the final payment was made, eleven thirty-something friends and two brand new twelve meter Benateau 39's were locked in for September '92.

Keeping such a large group enthused and up to date with developments was essential to keep the tempo up. Three members of the team lived in London; two lived in Sydney and the rest in Adelaide. To keep the morale high, we started a short newsletter with all the updates, logistics and photocopies of everyone's photos and favourite type of food. Some people were natural choices as key sailors, others volunteered to take charge of the galley and food supplies. We also had a registered nurse in the group, and one all-around "fix it" man with an interest in fishing.

To make the trip more cost effective and take advantage of being overseas, everyone organised their own adventures on either side of the sailing holiday. Two of us had a love of trekking and started looking for possible mountains to climb prior to the sailing. We found a Turkish trekking company that was offering trips to the Caucus Mountains in Russia. Others were planning a short trip to Egypt or stopping in Thailand on the way. We coordinated all of this by booking through the same travel agent. It was all an enormous headache, but Thor Travel in Adelaide made sure that everyone's flights coincided so we could meet within forty-eight hours of each other in Istanbul.

We completed our in-shore skippers' courses and finalised all the yachting documentation, organised our travel insurance, money, renewed passports and bought an easy guide to speaking Turkish. We packed our cosies, sun block, and two Australian flags.

On a winter's day in mid-August 1992, my friend Paul and I said farewell to our friends in Adelaide and flew off to Russia for our trek in the Caucasus. We were truly like water for chocolate, bubbling over with anticipation. It would be three weeks before we would meet them again in Istanbul. *"See you on the 4th"* they shouted as we walked onto the tarmac. The adventure was about to begin.

• • • • • • • ● ● ● • • • • • • •

It was very hot. From the lounge of the Sheraton Hotel in Istanbul, Paul and I sipped cokes and waited expectantly for Steve. The rendezvous was planned for two hours after our plane touched down and we were early. Our dusty rucksacks had been quickly stored out of sight by the porter. Three weeks in Russia had been exhilarating, our trek exhausting but very rewarding and now we were looking forward to some luxury. Steve and Katja had flown in from Thailand the day before with requests to find us a cheap but beautiful up-market hotel! We weren't disappointed. Over the next two days, as Rita and John flew in from Australia, and Sharon and

Claire joined us from Egypt, they all exclaimed in wonder. Our laughter and toasts were unstoppable as we relaxed and watched the red sun set over the Bosporus from our hotel's outdoor rooftop restaurant in the old quarter of Istanbul.

Turkey is a country full of noise and life. From daybreak, loud and mournful prayers resound from mosques throughout Istanbul, calling hundreds of Islamic Turks to pray. Cars toot and shops open spilling their wares onto sidewalks. Crowded buses muscle their way across the Galata Bridge linking the old and new city into a delightfully woven carpet of narrow alleyways, bazaars, and restaurants. And from every piercing, dark face came the similar greeting.

"Hey, lady - wanna buy a carpet? For you, best price! You Turkish? Spanish? Italian? Hey, wait...Where you from? Australia! Hey mate! Aussie! Kangaroo! You have a wonderful country! How long you stay? You like Turkey? You no buy - no problem. I wish you happy travels in my country. Enjoy! Safe journey!"

Heading south by public coach, we visited Gallipoli, Troy and Ephesus before arriving in Marmaris, the beautiful coastal port of the south coast. Million dollar yachts lay quietly sighing on their moorings awaiting their owner's next excursion. Yachties casually sauntered up and down the marinas with supplies, calling to each other and along the waterfront and dozens of outdoor restaurants spilled out over the water. The skies were blue with eight-knot breezes and the wine was chilled. We looked at each other and laughed. This was it.

Brigid, a former school friend of mine had flown in from London that morning with Sharon, a friend of hers, and Guy, who was a last minute ring-in. They were about to go swimming and were waiting for us on the sea wall, outside our pre-arranged hostel.

TS, my inner travel guide, is a very good judge of character and I felt her dig me in the ribs at the sight of this new man. He took my breath away with his soft tanned skin, fine brown hair that fell over his blue eyes and his strong, well-defined physique. Little did I know that seven years later, we would meet again and he would later become my husband and the father of our children but at that one moment, time stood still and all I could do was whisper *"wow"*. He smiled a shy hello and the introductions continued but my interest was aroused and the holiday took on an even more playful adventurous tone.

Pink geraniums cascaded over the balconies and were reflected in the candlelight as we all ate at al fresco that night, laughing and swapping stories of our travels, euphonically planning the next day's activities.

In the early hours before dawn, I awoke and stood at the open window. It was still dark. In the street below, two Turkish men laughed and bid each other goodnight as the local restaurant manager sighed and extinguished the light and closed the door. A dog barked somewhere far off in the town. Out over the water, the moonlight was bright, the harbour a mirror. Today was the day. Within a few hours, we would load up the yachts, check the equipment, pack our luggage into the cabins, fill the galley and set sail. As a skipper of one of the yachts, I was full of anxious expectation. I wondered about my skills, my navigation, what the weather would bring, how the team would get along and if we had enough chocolate. I simply couldn't relax.

Two years ago, who would have thought this was possible?

It was 4.00p.m. before we set sail. A lazy breakfast, official visit to Yuksell to check-in, a tour of the yachts, gear check, signing papers, and a mammoth grocery shopping spree including a very expensive box of Kellogg's Cornflakes, had taken up most of the day. Everyone helped, jumping into his or her voluntary roles. Guy had been designated to the other yacht, which needed more man power so I busied myself with the tasks at hand but always very aware of his presence.

The breeze was up and the skies were slightly cloudy as we headed out of the bay and turned north to explore the coast. The weather forecast seemed fine but before long, we were pushing into twenty six-knot breezes and the decks were wet. While the rest of us whooped in exhilaration, the non-sailors were looking very concerned! This was not what they had expected.

Consulting the chart, we saw a little bay 1-½ hours from Marmaris and headed in. The safety of the harbour was welcoming, and we motored slowly around looking for a good bottom on which to anchor and raft up together. When the yachts were finally settled, all of us felt relieved. With our baptism of fire over, we relaxed and officially announced the happy hour. That night, we started a cooking competition, which throughout the vacation would see three teams create some magnificent meals, often cooking on one yacht and climbing across or rowing the feast to the other yacht where everyone lay relaxing.

Over the next two weeks, eight-knot breezes and perfect blue skies enveloped us as we explored ancient ruins on foot, climbed hillsides to survey the Aegean and dined over lunch at ramshackle isolated restaurants eating fresh seafood. I never knew it then, but Guy was and still is allergic to fish. How he managed to survive without bringing it to the attention of everyone still amazes me but such is the measure of the man. Quiet, unassuming, soft-spoken, an engineer who quietly thinks problems through and appears never shaken, he is the opposite of me in many ways. Every yin does have a yang. I was intrigued and attracted to this quietly confident self-contained man but I wanted to see him laugh.

We were a cheeky and very playful group. When Claire discovered Guy's bright assortment of boxer shorts and distributed them for everyone to wear on board complete with erect bananas for a photo shoot, it did the trick. He took it well, there was laughter all around and I was hooked.

We sailed every day, swam, read, slept, played hilarious games, drank a lot and shopped until we dropped! At night we would visit tiny local restaurants, dance, have Turkish baths and talk insanely until the starlit skies left us speechless with their brilliance.

We met other yacht crews from around the world and a few times found ourselves amidst flotillas of up to twelve yachts sailing together. Often these were full of seemingly rich inexperienced landlubbers paying for the experience of sunbathing on the foredecks. We silently congratulated ourselves for going bareboat, which gave us so much independence and taught us so much about cruising.

Mooring the yachts in beautiful isolated coves where the cliffs plunge down into calm water, we would often drop anchor and reverse stern-first towards these cliffs, with long stern lines to the rocks. Then, untying the windsurfers and water toys, spend the whole afternoon in privacy. Beaches were wonderful for open wood fires at night as we sprawled on the sand beneath the stars, a place where holiday romances warmed and grew.

Every few days, we would come across villages to restock our grocery supplies, buy souvenirs and dine out. The information brochures and charts supplied by Yuksell were more than adequate for even novices like us and served as a great guide with suggestions on mooring positions and best anchoring spots. Daily radio contact with Yuksell and often-hilarious radio chats between the two yachts as they raced to the next cove kept us in touch with each other and the rest of the world.

Of course, some things did go wrong. Occasionally anchor lines got entangled and were caught under rock shelves. Once, while moored to a tiny jetty, the tide dropped overnight, leaving one yacht well and truly grounded while the other went in search of help. One sunny afternoon while lunching, anchored in the lee of a lovely island, one yacht began drifting quietly away! Plates went flying as six people dived into the water in pursuit! Tempers got frayed from time to time, but by the end of the first week, even the non-sailors had turned into winch wenches, were at the helm and were assisting with moorings and anchoring.

Our sailing skills increased immensely in those two short weeks. When I successfully moored our beautiful yacht back into its pen at the busy Marmaris marina with dozens of people looking on, there was a round of applause and I realised just how much we had all learnt. Smiles were a mile wide.

And what of friendship and the memories that bind us together? I am past the age of fairy stories and I am not in the habit of buying lottery tickets, but magical things do happen. Especially, when after all the dreaming, planning and hard work, friends abandon adult responsibilities and find the children in themselves once again. And as I felt my fears drift away into the Mediterranean sunlight and walked the pomegranate-stained sands of Selimye, I felt insanely happy. And the child in me? I hope she surfaces again soon. She was last seen frolicking unashamedly in those September seas.

Postscript

In 2016, my husband Guy and I organised a reunion sail for seven of our group, in the beautiful Hawkesbury, Pittwater region of Sydney on our own syndicated Hanse 38ft yacht. In the twenty-four years since that first memorable sailing holiday in Turkey, our group had experienced four marriages, one divorce and nine children had been raised. Now all aged in our fifties, the years melted away and we were immediately re-united again, joking, laughing, singing and sharing stories of those September Seas, forever bound together by our shared memories.

Mt Elbrus, Russia. 5,642 metres. The highest mountain in Europe.

We all dare to dream, but few of us dare to act. We spend our lives hesitating in the wings, instead of dancing on the stage of life.

Sorrel Wilby: Award winning Australian adventurer.
Author: *"Tibet, a Woman's Lone Trek Across a Mysterious Land"*

Mt. Elbrus's Skies

When I made the last few steps, I was suddenly invaded by emotions, laughing, crying, talking uncontrollably. Elbrus! At Last!

Brigitte Muir OAM. The first Australian to summit all Seven Summits.
Author: *"The Wind in my Hair"*.

"Julie, sometimes you've just got to say 'screw the pain - I'm, going to do this!'"

His concerned face was lost in a swirl of snow. A shiver rushed through me. High above us, Mt. Kasbek rose ominously resolute against the high altitude winds that raced across its summit. Everything was white.

I stood transfixed, unable to move up or down the ice wall. The toes of my crampons, which were taking my whole body weight, waited patiently for my decision. It had to come. In a moment of sheer madness and determination, I blinked the tears out of my eyes, gasped the thin air and headed up the wall.

It was August 18th, 1992. A brochure I had seen by chance had brought me here to Georgia in the Russian Caucasus Mountains. My friend who addressed me so inspiringly was Paul, my traveling soul mate with whom I had shared some amazing adventures. That day on the mountain we shared another - the summit of one of Russia's more remote peaks.

But at that one moment in time, as I was hanging precariously from my karabiner, tense against the icy blasts, I had to ask myself *"why the hell am I doing this?!!"* I should not have been so concerned, for the truism surely holds, those who persevere are often duly rewarded. One hour later, I reached the summit of Mt. Kasbek, the second highest summit in the Russian Caucasus mountains. At 5,033m, it was the highest peak that I had ever climbed.

So much for bravery. I couldn't see a thing. Through my thermal balaclava and insulated hood, I could hear the muffled wind buffeting my body. Spindrift flew in all directions. We were in cloud and everything was white. For two minutes we posed for photographs with the Australian flag whipped wildly in those icy gusts. I stood, blue lips framing a frozen smile, teeth chatting uncontrollably.

I don't remember descending the wall, but at its base, my body was racked with involuntary shivers. "Demar" our Russian Guide looked at me with concern, then pulled a spare jacket from his pack and placed it around my shoulders. The heat was instantaneous. I drank a litre of hot tea and ate three biscuits, our only food since 4.00a.m. that morning. I was dehydrated, ravenously hungry and felt weak. The break seemed to have the desired effect and soon my shivers subsided.

Gearing up again, we set off in single file tethered together with climbing rope, looped through the karabiners of our harnesses. The snow was shin deep, the slope perilously steep. Before long, the four leaders were leaping and bounding quickly downhill, eager to return to the hut. Being the shortest, I struggled to keep up, aware of the rope racing through my karabiner and waiting for the moment when I would be dragged screaming through the snow, suffocating as I was buried alive.

"Wake UP!!! Paul's call snapped me back to reality. Together we trekked the long miles back to the abandoned meteorological station and arrived at 5.30p.m. that night. Thirteen and a half hours on the slopes had left me utterly exhausted. I was angry for being left behind

by the guides and angry at the lack of food and advice. I wanted nothing more than to sleep, but inside, I was silently bursting with pride. I had made it.

The next morning I was bursting - literally. Having pushed my body well beyond its limits, it chose to voice its objections with an untimely menstrual cycle, which refused to quit. I was caught unawares with nothing to protect me but a stolen roll of thin Russian toilet paper. I made numerous trips to the outside dunny, a lean too, erected over a 300m abyss. At least the view was stunning. Flushing was out of the question. Our waste fell to the snowy slope far below and woe betide the poor trekker who chanced to choose that route. Of course, disposing of the thin paper was virtually impossible. Grimly I watched as the thin-soiled sheets sailed back up through the hole in the floor and flew humiliatingly around the dunny walls; staining everything it touched a lovely shade of pink. I didn't know whether to laugh or cry. Hiding my plight from the guys would be an impossible task.

We spent two more days at high altitude on Mt. Kasbek before the warmth of the valley beckoned us. It was an acclimatization climb and the isolation we had experienced if only for few days was ending temporarily. When I crossed the Gergeti glacier for the last time and left the perilous blue ice chasms behind me, I surprisingly felt a real sadness - the end of my first high altitude experience.

As we descended, we slowly encountered shrubs, then trees and finally forests. We passed villages and met local Russian people. Georgian farmers, their sickles sparkling in the sun, stopped their work and watched us silently from the fields as we trudged the last mile down to the village of Kasbek. The guys were dreaming of cold beers, and I, of western tampons.

I was a novice and had learnt my lessons the hard way. Within four days we would be back in the snow fields facing the biggest mountain of all and I was determined to not be caught unawares again. Our Russian leader was not one to offer advice and seemed unaccustomed to the eating habits of the west. I had to eat far more, dress much more warmly and carry more water to overcome dehydration. I humbly made peace with my body. Then I stocked up on complex carbohydrates, bought another large water bottle and second thermal jacket. I was ready to climb Mt Elbrus, the highest mountain in Europe.

• • • • • • • • ● ● ● ● ● ● • • • •

It was 3.00a.m. A crescent moon hung half way down the heavens. Far, far below us, lightning silently flashed across the valley, splitting the darkness like an eerie strobe light. I stepped from Pruitt Refuge onto the icy slope of Mt Elbrus and pulled on my over-mitts. Around me, a dozen or so climbers from around the world were whispering and chatting quietly, checking last minute gear before setting off. We were at 4,900m. There was no wind, just the crackling of ice beneath our boots. The frosty breath of climbers illuminated in the light from the refuge. It was my birthday, August 25th, and we were about to attempt the summit of the highest mountain in Europe.

We had arrived the day before, heavily laden with packs and food, via chair lifts, ski lifts and on foot. Mt Elbrus draws trekkers from many countries, eager to summit one of the seven highest peaks on the seven continents of the world. However, unlike the others, Mt Elbrus's slopes also attract skiers every winter, making the accent to base-camp at 4,900m reasonably easy.

From base-camp, Elbrus's twin summits arched to 5,642m above us in the clear night sky. We hoped to be on them by midday, which was an eight-hour trek away.

As each small party set off, I couldn't help but wonder what the day would bring. I was determined not to hold back the guys as I had on Mt Kasbek. I had made all my necessary precautions and I wanted to enjoy the experience. After all, it was my birthday. Roping up, we slowly set off in ankle deep snow, stepping in the footprints of those who had left ahead of us. It would be up all the way.

In his wisdom, Demar put me at the head of the line and took up second place. I felt burdened by the need to prove myself and took on the test before me. We set off.

High altitude trekking demands a very slow but steady rhythm. Breathe; lift leg, step-up, plant stocks. Breathe; lift leg, step-up, plant stocks....up and up the snowy slope. Stars twinkled miles above us. I could hear Demar breathing only inches from my ear, pushing me on. Higher and higher as we climbed in silence, we could hear the crackle of ice beneath our boots and our own rhythmic deep breathing. Determined not to stop and hold up the group, I forced myself through a steady rhythm. It soon became mechanical and I relaxed into the rhythm. I now began to enjoy myself, my muscles and breathing adapting to the game my mind was playing.

At 4.30a.m., on nearing some rocks high on the slope, I stopped, planted my stocks deeply into the snow and breathed a sigh of relief. Turning around to my surprise, I could find only Demar with me. Way down the slope in the moonlight, a dark group of tiny figures were sitting in the snow, exhausted. Elmar and Harry from Switzerland and my friend Paul had decided to take a break of their own. I exclaimed in surprise. I had been busting my boiler determined not to hold them up, thinking they were all right behind me full of energy! Perhaps I was going to make this after all!

Watching a sunrise at high altitude is about as close to God as I can get. Suspended between earth and sky, we danced with the cosmos as it dawned. The black blanket of night was slowly pulled back across the heavens and the sky softly awakened, pale at first, then bluer and bluer as friendly stars dissolved out of sight. Shades of orange bathed the clouds far below. Suddenly the sun burst its first rays over the curve of the earth and sent light splashing over the icy slopes. We looked around in awe. Above us, the deep blue disappeared into the universe, while far, far below, jagged mountain peaks rose majestically through the morning mists. Down there, people would be waking, making coffee and looking out of their windows up at the morning dawning. We were somehow removed from it all, isolated on our dazzling white slope that sloped forever upward.

Early morning toilet calls brought the reality of my mortality screaming home to me. I was in the middle of a dazzling snowfield surrounded by men with nothing but snow and ice around me for as far as the eye could see. There was nowhere to conveniently squat. I would either have to wait patiently or reveal all. I decided to wait until a revealing was needed.

The sun rose higher and we continued forever upwards. The international groups were all well dispersed by this stage and climbing steadily at their own pace stopping for breaks and eating from their personal stores of Russian chocolate and nuts. As we neared the lower of the two summit peaks near midday, the slope steepened dramatically so that our ice axes were always at the ready to catch us if we slipped. My face had turned a deep brown but I was feeling strong. Searing blue skies, no wind, warm and gentle breezes near the summit were making it a beautiful day. After my baptism of fire on Mt. Kasbek, Mt. Elbrus was a joy.

At 11.45 a.m. on August 25th, 1992, I celebrated my 30th birthday on the summit of Mt. Elbrus, Europe's highest mountain and my soul did truly fly. In that icy brilliant sunlight with dozens of snow-capped peaks that rose majestically from the clouds way below us, I felt I was in heaven. Standing 5,642m above the sea, above the valleys, above the villages, in the pure thin air, we were four black specks on the summit of the European world. Minutes lasted forever and our unabashed ecstatic chatter resounded in the silence. I collapsed playfully in the snow, while Paul piled me with birthday cards from home and took endless photos in the sunshine.

The trek back to Pruitt Refuge was very long and tiring and it was freezing cold, dark and sleeting heavily when we returned. Later that night, after we'd melted the ice from our clothing and hung our Polartec jackets and gloves up to dry, we joined two dozen other climbers around the fireplace in the kitchen hut, drank Russian vodka, ate chocolate and sang loudly, our sunburnt faces already starting to peel. I will never forget the generosity, laughter and genuine warmth and pride shared that night by madcap climbers in that Russian kitchen refuge while outside, the storm raged savagely in the darkness. Truly a thirtieth birthday to remember.

Volcan Villarica, Chile. 2,847 m.

*I am not one of those women who
trips twice over the same stone*

Isabel Allende: Chilean American Author: *"Ines of my Soul"*

Pucon – The Lake District of Chile

Get in the game. Play!
Just go and do that thing! TS

The morning sunlight was streaming through the coach windows when I awoke. The overnight trip south from the bustling Chilean capital Santiago had been comfortable and as my body tuned into the day, I could hear the first strains of South American guitars drifting through the coach's stereo system. I had awoken to a world of deep blue lakes and lush ancient forests, fresh and cool in the early morning mist.

As the sun rose higher, the coach meandered further south and soon there appeared between the trees; whitewashed two-storey German-style cottages with slate roofs and colourful window boxes. The air was crisp, the sun was shining and as far as the eye could see, forests, lakes, and snow-capped mountains appeared on the horizon. Suddenly the enormous breathtaking snow-cap 2,847-meter volcano Villarica appeared above the trees. I knew now, I had arrived in Pucon, one of the stunningly picturesque lakeside resort villages of Chile's Lake District.

I had one week to fill before travelling north to trek in the mountains on the Chilean/Argentinean border and was eager to spend my week relaxing amongst the best scenery that Chile had to offer. The Lake District was an unexpected find, a scenic playground of adventure that looked more German than South American.

The nineteenth-century German immigrants who started industries and populated the Chilean Lake District have left a strong influence on the architecture and food that still survives today, attracting not only many South American but foreign tourists as well. Known as Chile's adventure travel Mecca, the region attracts backpackers and tourists, couples and families, who want to participate in adventure sports and admire the views. Ten magnificent lakes reflect the mountains and dormant volcanoes of the eastern Andean Cordillera. Ancient cypress forests line their shores and fill the national parks of Conguillio, Tolhuaca, and Villarica.

Rolling into the village of Pucon by coach, my friends and I arrived at the main street, a quaint and picturesque place, which bustles with life as travellers eagerly book onto many adventure trips. Although I was yearning to relax quietly by the lake, TS and my friends Richard, Paul and Pina had other ideas and I was soon swept up by their enthusiasm. We spent four days experiencing the best of what Pucon had to offer.

I have always loved to climb. I love to stand above the clouds on a clear day surrounded by snow and spectacular views. Therefore, the thought of climbing Volcan Villarica really excited me. All equipment was provided for the one day trek to the summit. I looked up at the volcano and saw a thin plume of smoke swirl from its summit and prayed that Thor's anvil was out of action. However, after a day's delay because of rain and cloud, the mountain's plume of smoke disappeared and the sky dawned an unflawed blue. We met at 7.00a.m. at the tour office to be provisioned with the necessities like snow boots, crampons, gaiters, over pants, wind jackets, woollen hats, sunglasses, ski goggles and ice axes. Then, looking like "Michelin" men, we joined the other trekkers and with two mountain guides for support, we were driven up, up, up to the national park's ski resort to begin the climb.

The five-hour trek to the summit was on snow all the way and demanded a good level of fitness in order to cope with the higher altitude. Breathing heavily in the crisp air, and leaning on our ice axes for support, we slowly made our way higher and higher, a colourful string of wheezing, cherub-faced grinning tourists with high expectations. I was not disappointed. On reaching the summit, way above the clouds, the spectacular views of the region were mind-blowing and well worth the exhaustive climb.

The enormous live volcanic crater spat forth gasses, gurgles, and strange hisses rose from its depths, where Thor no doubt, was enjoying his day off. We spent forty minutes taking summit photos, laughing and snowball fighting before the icy wind encouraged a quick and exhilarating descent, which was rewarded with steaming chocolate and hot showers.

The next day, with Pina screaming in exhilaration inches from my ear, an enormous wave smashed against our raft, saturating us. I couldn't stop laughing. Having rafted white water in the Himalayas, we couldn't wait to sample the white waters of the Trancura and Turbio rivers. Not fans of icy water, though, we had chosen to wear wetsuits and helmets to ensure some warmth - and just as well. The mountain river was icy cold and our raft was ankle deep in water. We had booked with Anden Sports Tours however, we could also see competitor rafts belonging to Expeditions Apumanque and Trancura Expediciones Aventura. Exhilarating screams in countless languages were ringing through the gorges as the rafts dived and raced through the foam filled Trancura, leaving us very wet but safe at the hands of expert raft guides, who also provided beers and a BBQ at day's end.

Stretching, I could feel every muscle in my body. I had been working hard but within a day we hired mountain bikes and took off with day packs and a map, to explore the many forest tracks surrounding the lakes in the area. Finally, summiting a small hillock overlooking Pucon one afternoon, we collapsed on the grass in the sunshine, ate our picnic lunch and drifted into a heavenly doze surrounded by mountains, lakes, valleys and rivers.

That night was New Year's Eve, which the town celebrated with wild abandon and we found ourselves being dragged off the street into a restaurant and champagne being thrust into our hands. No one can party like those with a Spanish heart and the Chileans were pumping. With Latin rumbas blaring and conga lines weaving their way amongst the tables, we downed bottles of wine and joined the throng, dancing into the wee hours under a clear night sky.

As consciousness quietly seeped its way into my disorientated alcohol dazed mind the next morning, I could hear the patter of rain on the roof, which heralded a day of rest. In the early hours of the New Year, as the clouds rolled in, Volcan Villarica was covered in mist, and soft rain trickled down the window panes of our hostel. We had enjoyed three days of superb weather, exercise and a night of partying. The quiet day offered a tempting option to visit the natural thermal pools and hot springs set amongst the forests.

Alighting from the local bus in the rain that afternoon, we hitchhiked along dirt roads, enjoying the scenery. The natural springs were set deep in a forest, surrounded by log cabins. Dense steam rose from the hot bubbling water as we stripped quickly and slipped in up to our eyeballs, submerged hippos wallowing in the rain. By the time we climbed from the pools, hours later, our shrivelled bodies were hot prunes, the rain, like icicles. We hitched home with a lovely Chilean couple, Sonia and Martin. The journey was made even more memorable by sharing their local alcoholic "Bailey's" home brew, which was eagerly passed around the station wagon, causing much laughter as we chugged down the dirt road in the rain.

We had made full use of our time and too quickly it was over. Short breaks are often like that.

Although one is not inclined to be timid or nervous climbing mountains, it is nevertheless a trifle depressing to receive letters that say: 'If you are determined to commit suicide, why not come home and do so in a quiet lady-like manner?'

Annie Smith Peck: American mountaineer & trail blazing adventurer 1896

Basecamp Aconcagua, South America.
Highest mountain in the Southern Hemisphere. 6,961 metres

Memories of a Mountain

If you are not trying to climb a mountain in your life you
may never know what you can do or who you can be.

Brigitte Muir: OAM. First Australian woman to summit Mt Everest.
Author: *"The Wind In my Hair"*

"You have a large blood clot in your head. It's about four inches long and
as thick as a biro. It's blocking a cranial vein and the increased pressure and
swelling of your brain has stretched the nerve to your right eye, causing your
double vision. I'm afraid it's going to be a few months before your life will be
back to normal. You're very lucky it's not worse"

He continued but I wasn't listening. Bringing my hands to my temples,
I looked down at my body in the wheelchair. I closed my eyes to cut the
glare and try to stop the throbbing on the right side of my head that had
been causing me so much pain over the last three weeks.

Visions of the mountain came back to me. Deep blue skies, snow-
capped Andean peaks all around, brilliant sunshine, laughter and
smiles and then storms—always the wind howling, relentless, powerful,
frightening, threatening to blow us off the shoulder where we'd made
our camp at 5,300m. The blizzards so wild that our tents were ravaged
and buried time and time again. For forty-eight hours we dug and dug
ourselves free in sub-zero temperatures, day and night. The howling never
seemed to stop. What was it Sir Edmund Hillary had said about fear?

"Fear can be a stimulating factor. It can enable you to extend yourself far beyond what you thought possible. In any case, fear is all part of the motivation. If you don't feel afraid now and then, why go to all the discomfort and effort involved in getting up a high mountain? Better to stay sunbathing at the beach."

He was right. If I was not prepared to be afraid, I should have stayed at the beach. I had blown more than a few thousand dollars to try to climb to the summit of Aconcagua, the highest mountain in the world outside Asia and now was truly questioning my own sanity. None of it made sense to me. Why climb to an isolated world where nothing grows, no animals survive, where the oxygen is so thin that each step demands two long agonising breaths to sustain it? Why haul 30kg of gear up into a kingdom of gale force winds, where life is so tenuous?

But it had been beautiful - breathtakingly, spiritually beautiful, like the dawn of creation, before beast, before man. Between storms, when the clouds would roll back, they revealed a sky so deeply blue that the ice fields dazzled in its reflection, quickly burning any inch of skin left exposed to the frigid air. When the gales stop blowing at high altitude, the silence is humbling. Miles above the hustle of civilisation we sat alone, surrounded by blue ice, deep snow, craggy majestic cliffs and peaks with not a breath of sound. At night, the clear moonlit skies were pinned with millions of stars while peaks cast deep and silent shadows across our tents. There is a serenity and spirituality at high altitude that is palpable. Perhaps the sheer physical exhaustion of climbing there contributes to that sense of peace, for there is great satisfaction in physical achievement.

I was not a stranger to high altitude; however, reaching our high camp at 6,096m was a personal record for me. Not only had I climbed higher than ever before, but this time, without Sherpas, I had hauled my own gear all the way and reached my own personal summit.

But I am way ahead of myself. My story really began when seven friends decided it was time to stop simply dreaming about South America and actually go there. We learnt Spanish for months and worked out at the gym many times a week. I would climb the local Waterfall Gully to Mt. Lofty track in the Adelaide hills' dozens of times with stopwatch and backpack in readiness for the mountain. After five months of weight training, my 30kg backpack of telephone books and dumbbells was my best friend and my eating habits resembled those of a prize fighter. My shapely legs were as hard as iron and my 60kg frame had buns of steel and was the fittest it had ever been. Aerobically, there was no stopping me. There was no doubt in my mind that I was ready.

On arrival in South America in January 1995, while my friends enjoyed the vistas of Buenos Aires, Iguazu Falls and Bolivia, I headed off to Santiago with my friend Paul. We were to join an Alaskan trekking party, *"Aventuras Patagonicas"*, to climb Mt. Aconcagua. At 6,959.8m it is the highest mountain in the southern and western hemispheres and the highest mountain in the world outside Asia. It is one of the seven highest mountains on the seven continents of the world.

Our Alaskan expedition consisted of twelve men and me. However, a few days before departure, our chief guide Rodrigo, sprained his ankle and was replaced by Nancy, a blond, slim, attractive thirty-five year old Alaskan mountain guide who in her spare time, led sea kayaking expeditions in Patagonia, para-sailed and had built her own log cabin. The rest of the team consisted of three Australians, seven Alaskans and two support guides, who were to work with Nancy. I was surrounded by a team of strong, strapping men, capable of hauling enormous loads many miles in knee-deep snow and never flinching in the face of fear. My puny frame seemed to be somewhat inadequate but I was consoled by the fact that Nancy's physique was very slight and identical to mine in build.

If this woman could lead this macho expedition, then I could certainly follow. I was determined to keep up and not cry under any circumstances. While my plutonic mate Paul made friends with Nancy, I befriended Ron, the biggest and strongest Alaskan guy in the team.

We set out from Santiago, north to the Andes where we met the mule train that would haul our gear to base camp at 4,267m. The towering cliffs and barren outcrops of the Relinchos and Vaccas Valleys open to high desert vistas coloured only by pockets of tiny wildflowers, clinging to life. The Australians coped well in the heat, but as the days passed and we climbed higher and higher up the mountain ridges, the Alaskans forged the way.

Base camp was established on a rocky scree slope. Bright, yellow tents flapped wildly buffeted by icy winds. We buried our guy ropes beneath massive rocks to keep them in position and Paul and I busied ourselves, building a fortress of rocks around our tent to protect it from the wind.

Then the weather turned, bringing with it deep snow, black skies and deafening gales screeching up to 85km an hour. Within forty-eight hours, our yellow tents on the once barren and rocky Relinchos glacier were buried beneath a meter of snow, unheard of for that time of year. Over the next few days, trapped at base camp, we enjoyed the camaraderie of a climber's life, visiting the other expedition tents and talking to climbers from around the world.

Meeting and sharing a cocoa and conversations with Brigitte Muir, leader of the Australian Expedition and Australia's finest female mountain climber was inspiring. As she enthusiastically discussed her hopes to be Australia's first female climber to summit Mt. Everest later in the year, my hopes for summiting Aconcagua rose. Little did we know that she would go on to fulfil her dreams and be awarded an OAM for her contributions to Australian mountain climbing.

The next day I enthusiastically hauled one load through deep snow to camp one at 4,877m - only to lumber back to base camp in sleet. A few days later, when the threat of avalanches had subsided, we set off again, climbing to camp two at 5,300m just as the clouds moved in again.

For seventy-two hours we were trapped in tents, except for the daily non-negotiable call of nature that forced us to brave the gales and spin drift to bare our butts in intolerable freezing conditions. Urinating was another matter. To combat severe dehydration, up to six litres of water a day was required, leading to a continuous need to relieve oneself. Pee bottles became a necessity easily used by men. However, as a woman, squatting, short of breath in cramped unisex tents, is a feat in itself. It demands skill, balance, and utmost trust! Many female mountain climbers have mastered the funnel and pee bottle-balancing act while stooping over in a tiny snow-laden tent. I am not one of those women. Despite having practiced the funnel approach many times in a warm shower, doing it at 5,300m in freezing conditions was a tragically humourless affair.

We would pass the tedious hours snug in our sleeping bags, talking, continuously, eating and drinking, and melting snow for water bottles while the storms raged outside. Books were torn in half, circulated and read by headlamps at night while listening to the roar of avalanches as they raged down nearby gullies. At the height of the storm, we would rotate through four hourly shifts, despondently leaving warm sleeping bags in the dead of night to endure the howling gale and dig snow by torch light in minus thirty degree temperatures. Without it, tents could easily have collapsed or become so buried that the oxygen supply was blocked off.

When the storms cleared and we set forth from camp two at 5,300m, we had used all our spare food supplies. We were faced with a 762m climb through mountains of snow, bypassing camp three, straight to camp four where we would make our summit attempt. If we were lucky, we could do it in eight hours. If the weather turned again, we could be climbing for 13 hours or more.

The morning was crisp, clear and sunny, but there was an ominous feeling amongst the group. The challenge ahead was enormous and each of us harboured our own personal fears as we set out that day with fully laden packs and enough reserve energy, we hoped, to get us through the day. High altitude climbing is exhausting. Fear, pain, negativity and extreme discomfort are never far away, beckoning and coaxing the climber to turn back, to give up. The power to get to the summit rests solely with each individual. It is a constant test of willpower, a personal quest to win.

That January morning, breathing heavily in the thin air, we hauled our packs onto our backs, adjusted the straps and ski poles and slowly, very slowly, started the long trek upwards. With each step, we stopped to breathe twice in an unending rhythm that would carry us through the day. The spindrift swirled around each footprint and I soon fell mesmerised into my own private world, following the mythical Good King Wenceslas as he led me through the snow.

By the time we neared camp four we had been climbing steadily for eight hours in the icy wind and shin deep snow. Good King Wenceslas had long been replaced by a new mantra of Gloria Gaynor's exasperating disco hit "I Will Survive". With the end in sight, a seemingly easy one-kilometre traverse to Camp Four had led us straight into a vast and terrifying *Penetentes* field. Penetentes are hip high slivers of knife-like edges of ice that stick up from the ground. These are formed as the snow melts around them and are difficult to climb through. Now after storms, they were covered in snow and invisible to the eye, making them dangerous as well. When Chris, our support guide yelped in pain and sank to his waist in the Penetentes field, we knew we would have to descend and re-climb the slope from another angle.

Frustration and tears threatened to overcome me but there was no alternative. Though exhausted, we trekked back down to 5,500m then once again began the slow climb to 5,950m. Four hours later, as we neared camp, I knew my will power was gone. My 30kg pack may as well have been 100kg and the straps were cutting deeply into my shoulders, doubling me over. The unending rhythm of stepping up and breathing, stepping up and breathing was agonising but constant and had carried me through the day, but now I was on an autopilot. I simply did not have the energy or the will to care anymore. I didn't care about the mind-blowing views or the icy wind or all the pain. Nothing mattered except getting to camp where I could rest. Tunnel vision set in as all my concentration focused on the footprints leading me to camp.

Twenty meters from camp four, I slowly realised that my left hand was frozen. It had been holding my ski pole on the high side of the mountain as we traversed and the blood had drained out of it freezing it into a clenched fist around the handle of my stock. Suddenly, my hypnosis disappeared.

Now fully aware of the intense pain in my hand, fear flooded through me. Forgetting everything, I wildly shook and shook my hand to start the circulation. Despite my previous promise to myself, I couldn't hold back and the involuntary tears started to flow. An enormous floodgate opened and before I could stop myself, I fell to my knees in the snow, hugging my hand to my chest, huge sobs racking my entire body, my ski goggles filling with tears. I couldn't get up. I had hit the wall.

As evening set over the mountains, we all watched exhausted as the clouds teasingly parted and beautiful salmon pink rays of sunlight danced across the snow-capped precipices before being engulfed by clouds. Ron had hauled my pack the last 20m to camp. His reassuring smile, jokes and encouragement had saved my sanity, but inside I knew I could go no higher in such weather.

In the early hours of the morning, as the summit team packed to leave, I stood shivering in the silence, full of anticipation. I wondered what the day would hold for my friends. The night sky was clear and bright moonlight bathed the peaks and valleys' miles below. The wind had disappeared.

None of us made it to the summit. As the day unfolded, the storms returned. Gales, sub-zero temperatures, and zero visibility engulfed Paul and the other three climbers with enough reserve energy to attempt it. At 6,400m the danger had become too great and they turned back, 561m short of their goal. They returned to camp, mute from exhaustion and defeat. I spent summit day in my sleeping bag, listening to the gales that had begun around dawn, reluctant to move, dreaming of gleaming white bathrooms, hot showers, porcelain toilets, shampoo and fluffy towels. We miss the little things in life the most.

The next day, we left the frozen world behind us and in one day, descended through deep snow, down the steep and quickest route, 3,000m into the public trekker's base camp on the other side of the mountain. It was a virtual town of tents from every country on the globe. We booked into a wooden chalet, had relaxing hot showers for the first time in two weeks, slept on comfortable warm bunk beds, and ate hearty meals as other climbers prepared for their ascent.

Again I was faced with the question of why. What drives sensible, rational people to push themselves to the absolute limit to experience such beautiful yet hostile wilderness at the expense of health and wealth? For some climbers, the summit drives all their energy to succeed, but they are often blind to the journey. For others, the climb itself is the challenge to be savoured, the bonding and camaraderie of climbers a gift, the scenery to be long remembered. For some, it is ego, a crusade for devilish photos and the ability to boast and fulfil their lust for adventure. They will return again and again to conquer and to win.

I climbed because I wanted to see if I had what it took to stand on the summit of the highest mountain in the southern and western hemispheres.

I got sick soon after our descent. While, my friends were on holiday in the mountains of Peru, surrounded by every woman's bargain shopping dream, I was experiencing violent fits of nausea, migraines, and double vision. The doctors assured me it was nothing but acute altitude sickness that would disappear when I reached sea level. As we had planned a glamorous two-week bare boat yacht charter in Tahiti to end the holiday, I looked forward to a quick recovery and to bask in the sun on the yacht off the coast of Bora Bora. But it wasn't to be. I was confined to bed for the entire week, the only consolation being the bevy of attractive French doctors in Tahiti who attended to me.

I arrived back in Adelaide, two weeks earlier than expected and was hospitalised, only to discover my mountain sickness had camouflaged a more sinister companion brought about by dehydration and use of the pill at high altitude. Six months later, my eyesight recovered and my blood clot dissolved enough for doctors to assure me I would live to 100 but my high altitude mountaineering days were perhaps over.

Looking back, I have long since forgotten the pain and the smell of unwashed two-week-old thermal underwear. And instead, my memories bring a gentle calm resolve, which comes from facing and overcoming personal fear and touching the fragility of life.

I have been fortunate to meet mountaineering men and women from Australia and Alaska. I have interviewed some in crowded hotel rooms sitting cross-legged on beds surrounded by expedition equipment; sitting at rough wooden benches clasping cocoa discussing the logistics and weather patterns facing the climb; huddled cosily at night in small tents at 5,500m while avalanches raged down nearby gullies. Later, when the hurly-burly was done, I have sat in suburban homes surrounded by enlarged summit photos of beaming faces on top of Aconcagua, Elbrus, Denali, Kilimanjaro, Vinson, Everest and Kosciuszko: the seven summits.

All these men and women were happy, strong, independent and full of life. They were inspirational. Some women had young babies at home and were facing the struggles of juggling motherhood and their love for climbing. Some of them were professional climbers, others simply on leave from the office to experience the joys and fears of high altitude. Some were slight of build, feline, and delicate. Others were physically robust, obviously strong and capable. All were mentally powerful, determined and entertaining.

In a sport, where physical and mental strength is a prerequisite, gradually more women, in particular, are discovering these faculties in themselves. As climbers, they are juggling motherhood, households, careers, menstrual cycles, funnels and pee bottles at high altitudes. They are proving that both men and women with physical and mental strength can climb any summit, for power lies within each of us, regardless of gender. We are so lucky to be living at a time when both men and women are free to choose.

No matter how long you train someone to be brave, you never know if they are or not until something dangerous happens

Veronica Roth, American Author: "Divergent"

Indian Adventure

Courage doesn't always roar. Sometimes
courage is the little voice at the end of the
day that says 'I'll try again tomorrow'

Mary Anne Radmacher, American Author: *"Lean Forward into Your Life"*

It was sweltering hot. Perspiration dripped from Paul's face as he squinted into the sun, his eyes watching the bus, now a speck on the horizon. The dust settled quietly around us. *"Paul, our rucksacks were in the back"*.

My words seemed to hang in the heat. A bird squawked in laughter in a tree to our left, but the situation was really very far from funny.

Along the roadside, old men and brightly clad Indian women were running away dragging their crying children. The high pitched sound of their panic-stricken voices rang clear in the afternoon air. Fallen produce from their baskets littered the dusty road. We were suddenly alone.

Our minds are amazing things. Even though deep inside I knew the reality, instinctively, I looked around for a camera crew, wondering if we were in the middle of an elaborately well-orchestrated prank. Any minute I expected a director to yell 'cut' and for dozens of people to appear, laughing at our shocked faces. I laughed nervously. It was surreal.

We had been travelling for hours on an over-crowed Indian bus, a forty eight hour journey down steep mountain roads through the Himalayas from Kathmandu to Delhi. We had been packed into the bus like sardines, shoulder to shoulder, thigh to thigh. The diesel fumes, searing summer heat and body odours were strong and diffused only by the dusty hot breeze that would swirl in through the open windows as we would career around dangerous curves. The monotonous drone of the engine and endless bumping to and fro had rocked most people to sleep. I smiled at a three-year-old Indian girl astride her mother's lap, perspiration dripping down her pretty face, her large black eyes staring at me. Her hair lay damp, strands stuck to her beautiful olive brown skin. She held a half-eaten banana in her hand. She began to smile at me and then in an instant, everything changed. Suddenly, the bus swerved to the left sending us all sprawling against the dirty windows. Then over-correcting, we were tossed to the other side as the driver swerved back to the right. I remember screams and dust choking us as the bus crashed and stopped.

Falling through the open doors with the throng, we moved to the center of the road; I squatted to inspect the dark pool of blood that was quickly being absorbed into the dust. Soon, with the afternoon heat and flies, it would disappear. So much blood.....

"Don't look," Paul said. *"Let's just get out of here"*

I checked my money and passport and realised with relief that I had my camera with me. All the essentials, except water. But everything else we owned was now tearing at a hectic rate away from us and to where?

Kicking at the dust, out T-shirts discolouring with sweat, we decided to follow the throng, now a long drawn out line of stragglers on the horizon. Soon they disappeared altogether. *"Like Hansel and Gretel following the breadcrumbs,"* I thought as we followed the dark trail of blood that had gushed from the bus. After half a kilometre, it narrowed to a trickle and disappeared completely. Still, the road continued. As the day wore on, the temperature soared.

There was nothing but fields, a few trees, and the silence of a hot afternoon, coupled with no water and the dirt road was unnerving. Paul's mood was turning shitty. *"Where the hell are we anyway?"* We were covered in sweat and dust and in need of a village well. (Actually, a hotel, cold beer, cool shower and restaurant would have been perfect.)

The creaking of worn tyres against buckled bicycle rims broke the silence of the afternoon. It wobbled towards us, pulling a cycle rickshaw. The driver was old and very thin. His skin had withered dark brown from years in the harsh Indian sunshine. He stopped and smiled a toothless smile, beckoning to us in Hindi, to get on.

"We must be near a village. Can you take us to the police station?" Paul asked.

"You know, POLICE very important men, bang, bang, salute," he said as he wildly gestured, his arms imitating shooting pistols.

"Do you understand??" Paul asked in frustration.

"We want to go to the POLICE!"

The old man's face broke into another wide toothless grin as he enthusiastically nodded his head from left to right, left to right in the traditional Indian manner.

"That means yes," I said to Paul.

"I think he's got it".

We got on. As the rickshaw made a very slow "U" turn and wobbled dangerously as the old man stood to cycle, every bone in his old tired body straining to pull our 130kg.

"I'm worried he'll have a heart attack," I said.

But the driver was strong and soon our wobbling rickshaw was in sight of a small village of ramshackle huts. Happily, pulling up at a broken down railway station, the driver turned and grinned and held his hand out for payment.

"No-no the POLICE! We want to go to the POLICE station" said Paul, saluting and firing off another round into the air in exasperation.

Recognition spread across the old man's face. Forty-five minutes later, having visited a post office, a shop, and a sleazy hotel, we approached a dirty cream-coloured building where an official looking man lazed, smoking in the shade of the veranda. Our driver was now dripping wet with perspiration and had lost his grin. Grateful, we handed over the $3 and a big tip and with a smile, he disappeared down the road, his wheels leaving soft tracks in the dusty street.

Indian summer evenings are long and warm. They bring beguiling blood red skies as the sun slowly sinks below the horizon. It is one of the nature's special gifts to mankind, a beautiful and peaceful sight. But that long warm evening, as we waited for the constable to return on his spluttering motorcycle with news of the accident, was far from charming. We had been waiting on the veranda for four hours and it was getting dark. We had not eaten, had nowhere to sleep and no luggage.

We could hear the spluttering motorcycle approach before we saw its dim headlight. The constable sauntered up to the steps towards us, nodded and entered the office to speak with his superior. An intense discussion in Hindi followed. Beckoning us into the dingy office, the superior officer smiled and in broken English intimated that no bus accident had been reported or was known of by any of the locals. However, a man was in the hospital, who had hurt his head but would be fine by morning. He knew nothing about our luggage.

Paul's face turned red with frustration and anger.

"There WAS a bus accident, I tell you and the man is not in hospital, he is DEAD!! He doesn't have a head! It was splattered all over the road! He was leaning out the window when the other bus swiped us and took it right off.

We saw his body. It was hanging out of the bus without a head. Why the hell don't you believe us?"

"No, no, no. I tell you he is in hospital and is all right".

The constable was defensive and embarrassed now. The two men stood aggressively as they faced each other, with Paul tense, angry and travel worn, and the constable contradicted and humiliated in front of his superior officer. The contrast in stories was too humorous to even laugh about. The room was silent.

"You return in the morning please" the superior officer intimated.

"No more tonight".

Frustrated and exhausted we left the office and headed for the sleazy hotel. That night, as I lay, perspiring on my sagging stained sheetless mattress, my thoughts returned to Nepal. Only one week ago we had been trekking across what seemed like the roof of the world, above clouds, amidst green meadows and blue skies. Instinctively, I looked across at Paul on the next bed. He was lying on his back, a tired arm swatting mosquitoes that had intercepted the holes of the mosquito net that hung from the roof. What a holiday. We had heard that entering India from Nepal via the backdoor route was a rough trip but this was too much.

"Tomorrow we'll get our bags and catch the first bus we can to Benares and book into a plush hotel... with a pool, room service, and hot showers... we deserve it," I thought as sleep overtook me.

Sometime later that night, I awoke nauseous and wet with perspiration. I couldn't get over the shocking accident. Visions haunted me.

The crowded bus, vegetables, live ducks and market produce, smiling Indian women and the laughing faces of their children and then swerving, men yelling, an awful grating sound as the buses collided and the screech of brakes as the driver brought it to a stop. I had looked around for Paul, lost in the sea of faces at the back of the bus but couldn't see him. People were shoving and yelling and children were crying. Falling out of the doors with the throng, I had crossed to the other side of the road. Bewildered, I looked back at the bus. I had never seen a dead body before. Hanging headless from the broken window it looked like.....meat. A fountain of blood poured from the gaping hole where a head should have been. His clothes were stained dark red. One arm had also disappeared.

I got up to open the window to breathe what little breeze swirled in the Indian night. As I switched on the light, a dozen panicking cockroaches scrambled under the bed. I leaned over the dirty sink and wretched. I realised I smelt awful. Falling back into bed, I thought of the mountains and wondered what my heroines would have done.

Two days later, we were again summoned to the dirty cream office of the superior officer. Hours of killing time and waiting had left us despondent. We wanted to leave, rucksacks or no rucksacks.

"I have good news for you". His face beamed proudly above his sweat-stained collar.

"Early this morning we find your bags and bus in a large shed. The man yes is very, very dead. No good. There, take your bags."

True enough, our bags, covered in dust, lay thrown on the floor. Although mine was intact, Paul's padlock had been smashed. His camera lenses had disappeared. A good thing about Paul is his wonderful ability to see the humorous side when none exists. Now, realising our ordeal was very nearly over and we had survived unscathed, he simply shrugged resigned to the fact that he hoped the new owner possessed a Canon SLR camera for without it, the lenses were useless.

"What you mean useless?" replied the constable.

"Is no good?"

"They're useless without the camera".

"What kind of camera? Show me" the constable urged.

"Sure and while we're at it can you write a letter for my insurance company to say the lenses were stolen please?" asked Paul.

"No, no, not stolen, LOST" replied the superior officer.

"But it was stolen; see, the lock has been smashed"

"No, no LOST, only LOST" came the reply.

Resigned to the fact that perhaps someone other than lowly poor Indian farmers had tampered with the bag, Paul gave up the fight. Accepting the scrawled letter, sealed proudly with the official seal of the Indian police, we stepped out into the sunshine and headed for the dusty highway to flag down the first vehicle going south.

But in India, more adventures are always around the corner. It had been a fascinating trip. And we couldn't help wondering what the rest of the holiday would bring.

Tea Pluckers: Sri Lanka

*Ebrace your past, then grasp your
future with grateful hands.* TS

Return to my Emerald Isle

When you're traveling with someone else, you share each discovery, but when you are alone, you have to carry each experience with you like a secret, something you have to write on your heart, because there's no other way to preserve it.

Shauna Niequist: American Author: *Bread and Wine*

When I was twenty-two years old, I backpacked for nine months, exploring Britain, Europe, Morocco, Nepal, India, Sri Lanka and the Maldives. While in Scotland I hired a car and spent a fabulous two weeks, driving from youth hostel to youth hostel, shrouded in rain and mist, buffeted by icy winds. The warmth and camaraderie of other backpackers braving the weather and singing in front of roaring fires at local country pubs was truly memorable.

I traced our 'Robertson' name to Fort William, found our Scottish family tartan and marvelled how, during the Jacobean uprising, the Robertson Clan had assisted Bonny Prince Charlie to flee over the sea to the Isle of Skye. I learnt the famous "Skye Boat Song" and how Flora MacDonald, a courageous twenty-four year old woman had led the rescue dressed as an Irish maid-servant to ensure the safe passage of the young Prince. She must have been extremely brave.

I feel a strong link to Scotland and love its mind blowing spiritual beauty and the fact that my ancestors were proud highlanders.

The Robertsons joined the British Burgher community in Ceylon where they remained for three generations - a big railway clan of train drivers, railway super-intendants, foreman, plate laying overseers, railway inspectors, and a naval officer, living an expatriate lifestyle in the Emerald Isle. They lived in the hill country and on the coast, amongst manicured gardens, wearing British linen suites somewhat detached from the simple life of the local people. This is the family heritage into which I was born.

And so on Thursday, 12th December 1985, I returned to Sri Lanka and touched down at Colombo International airport to make sense of it and to touch my past.

In my backpack, I carried the names and addresses of Sri Lankan people and places that had played a part in my history. My singular mission was to find them, to see the houses, the jungles, the markets and the schools where my parents grew up, fell in love, and the hospital of my birth. But in those first few moments, as I stepped onto the tarmac, I was overcome with tears to be on the terra firma of my birth.

I had left Ceylon (as it was called in those days) with my parents, twenty-one years earlier on the ocean liner, *The Canberra*, bound for Australia – a wide-eyed two year old, holding hands with her older brother and hiding in the folds of her mother's skirt.

Colombo airport was refreshingly efficient, clean and hassle free. The previous two harrowing weeks that I had endured in the Indian countryside, surviving a dramatic bus accident, lost luggage and days of frustration, all paled into insignificance. In Colombo, the sun was shining. The Sri Lankan customs officers smiled at me and waved me through passport control and suddenly I was on the street. In no time, having consulted our guidebook, my travelling companions Paul, Scott and I were booked into the Mt Lavinia Tropic Inn.

That first evening in Colombo, I excused myself from the guys and took a long walk along Mt Lavinia beach alone. I felt amazingly happy. This was the very same spot where my parents had dated and walked together so many years before my birth.

I sat alone and watched the sun set unaware of a young local boy watching me. He soon plopped himself next to me, squatting on the sand. At his feet was a closed woven basket. Smiling widely at me he took out a punji flute from the folds of his sarong and began playing. He drew an instant response from a huge cobra that rhythmically rose from the basket, inches from my knee, swaying to the melody. Startled, I jumped backwards to the laughter of the young boy who held out his hand for a few rupees which I happily handed to him.

After Paul and Scott returned to Australia, I travelled solo throughout Sri Lanka on trains, busses, and trishaws, visiting the sites that I had grown up hearing about. I hired drivers as guides and stayed in small guest houses to enjoy the sensory overload that my cousin Hazel had captured so beautifully to entice me:

> "Green that is intensely lush and deep; smiling people; laughing happy children; coconut, banana and paw-paw fruit trees; the beautiful rolling Kandy hills; cool mornings and warm tropical afternoons; the unexpected thunderstorms and lightening that make you quake; long train rides from Kandy to Colombo; people who speak three languages; white teeth, toothless smiles....

> ...power cuts; water shortages; poor people trying to earn enough for a meal; the beggars, young and old; a woman selling fruit at the market with her new born baby in a cardboard box; shop owners calling "hello, hello, come, come, look, look.....

> ...the proud rich upper-class; the bribing, the abuse of power; the need to impress;, the temples; ash on the foreheads of the Hindus; the call to prayer from the Muslim mosques at the crack of dawn; the lighting of oil lamps under the bow trees next to the statue of the Buddha; the Christian children in their white

school uniforms; a young boy of twelve working hard, leading his elephant; the monkeys climbing the temple walls….

….the tri-shaw taxis, weaving in and out of the traffic; women with long dark hair in colorful sarongs going for their daily bath to the well or river, gossiping and laughing; the tantalizing delicious smells and tastes of the curries and rice; chilli, chilli, chilli in everything; delicious sambals, wonderful cooks; genuine hospitality."

On a remote jungle track, I searched for the house from which my young mother, heavily pregnant with me, had waddled to the local hospital. As I am from a large family clan who had lived in the area for many years, I stopped at a house by the jungle's edge and inquired if they knew of my grandparents and if I was going in the right direction. Surprised, the boy beckoned me toward the house, calling to his mother who on seeing me for the first time, immediately claimed me as a long lost relative. I was. Unbeknown to me, my mother had written to her cousin saying that I would be in the country, never suspecting that I would inadvertently stumble upon their home. I was immediately invited to stay and spent the next few days cocooned in their care. Joyce and her husband Victor were wonderful hosts, introduced me to my heritage, shared long family stories and showed me family sites throughout the surrounding hill towns.

We bathed daily at the local well, ate rice and curry, talked of family and of Australia and visited the building where I was born. Nuns now run the Centre that has become a home for local Sri Lankan girls. Amused and excited by my inquiry, one of the nuns went to the attic and brought down an enormous hospital register. Turning to 1962, we slowly scanned the dust covered faded pages and there it was in blue ink, scribbled handwriting, my mother's name, aged 24 years and the date and time of my birth.

I immediately burst into uncontrollably happy tears, which lasted for some time, much to the amusement of the girls and nuns who hugged and laughed and giggled and smiled. To have returned to the place of my birth at age twenty-two and imagine my mother right there as a young woman of the similar age giving birth to me was a surreal moment. I left Sri Lanka a few days later, with a profound sense of being a product of a long and intertwined web of history that dates back hundreds of years. Somewhere in my past, a relative had fought for the bonny prince. Looking down at the register in Padiwatte, Sri Lanka, in the long shadows of the afternoon sun, I was at last in touch with the past that was no longer mystical but tangible.

Postscript

Thirty years later, I returned to Sri Lanka with my parents, my husband Guy and our children Jordon and Lauren, on the 50th anniversary of our emigration to Australia. Together, mum and dad showed my husband and children the beauty of our island paradise. I watched in wonder as they once again told their stories and laughed and cried as we travelled our beautiful island together. My son Jordon captured their emotions and stories on video so that future generations will know what they endured, how they lived, what they sacrificed and how we came to be.

*The African sunsets were
lovelier than words can say; the
crimson glow catching the snows
of Kilimanjaro, turning the sky
blood-red. Even the natives were
struck with the beauty of it.*

Lady Genesta Hamilton: British adventurer,
Author: *"A Stones Throw"*

Meeting the Maasai

*You know you are truly alive
when you're living among lions.*

Baroness Karen Blixen, Danish adventurer, Author: *"Out of Africa"*

Staring down into the battered saucepan, I watched the donuts sizzle. It was a special treat for a hungry band of twelve weary travellers. It was Sharon's idea and she was on meal duty. Busily clearing the collapsible wooden table and wiping off the dust, she held one of the tin plates up to the sun and inspected it carefully. Wiping it across the seat of her pants she looked at me, grinned and shrugged. It would have to do.

I smiled to myself. Only one week before, she had left her corporate life behind and had stepped for the first time, onto Third World soil. The culture shock had been great. Overwhelmed, she tried to hold back her tears in the muddy bus station at Arusha, Tanzania as she had looked at me with a hint of wild fear. It was not what she had expected. Dozens of very black Africans standing barefoot in the mud, draped in bright reams of cloth watched us through the drizzle. Loud voices called out the prices of bus fares and unfamiliar sounds and smells surrounded us. Women, balancing market produce on their heads, walked the muddy streets clutching inquisitive children. We had arrived solo with just our rucksacks and rough directions to the Arusha hotel where we would meet our expedition group.

"Whatever you do, don't lose me in the crowd" her eyes had pleaded. I knew she was serious.

Now, under bright blue African skies and a burning sun, I admired how she was coping. The nail polish and makeup were gone. One week of camping had left her khaki shorts grimy and her loose denim shirt was crumpled and stained, but her face now held wide enthusiastic smiles and carefree laughter the deeper we ventured into the Serengeti. She was in her element!

She flipped the donuts. The upbeat sound of UB40's "Rats in the Kitchen" suddenly exploded from the stereo of the Bedford truck. Chris, our driver, appeared grinning from behind the cab. *"Let's get this party going,"* he said bopping and peeping curiously into the pan. Sharon playfully wrapped him on the knuckles and pushed him out of the makeshift kitchen.

We were camped on a grassy hillside. The Serengeti Plain stretched for miles in all directions, its long straw grass waving in the hot afternoon breeze. It was a lazy day and other members of the team were relaxing, milling around the truck in the shade, reading or sitting chatting and trying to escape the heat. As the music picked up, so did everyone's spirit. One by one, toes began tapping and bodies started to bop. We were miles from anywhere and in the quiet stillness of the hot afternoon, our voices and music were loud.

Before long, Chris appeared again, grinning widely. *"You've got to see this,"* he said. We followed him inquisitively. Not six meters away, we could see a small group of Maasai warriors standing in their characteristic one-legged stance, spears in hand, the sole of their left foot firmly balanced against the side of their right knee. To our surprise, they were swaying to the music, their white perfect teeth smiling brightly in their black faces. They returned our welcome with happy nods but kept their distance, watching us closely, obviously enjoying the beat. Everyone was now watching in anticipation, wondering what would happen next. A few of our team started to dance and invited them to join in. To our surprise, although they kept their distance, the Maasai laughed, and like children learning a new dance, shyly indulged in copying some western movements, raising their spears to the beat.

They were dressed majestically in vibrant colours. Their purple robes were regal and fell from one shoulder to the shin. Around their necks were brightly woven handmade circular disks of brilliant colours, which matched with their armbands, worn high on their arms. Long, colourful earrings fell to their shoulders. Their shaven heads and clear skinned faces were deep brown from the sun and glistened slightly with perspiration from the heat. They wore sandals.

During the next two weeks, we would meet many more Maasai and speak in universal sign language with them, exchanging information and smiles and trinkets. They would often appear silently, inquisitively watching us and just as suddenly disappear. We would learn how their children, on entering their presence, would first bow their head and await a light touch on their forehead before venturing to speak, as a sign of deep respect. We would come across villages and see their straw and dung-covered huts, full of smoke from their wood fires and hear about the diseases that troubled them. We would talk to Maasai goat herders about their lifestyle and the magic fire mountain, Kilimanjaro, that they revered. We would hear about their goat's milk, mixed with urine that they drank daily and marvel at how, amidst the squalor of their villages, they kept so clean and proud and regal.

The Maasai stayed with us that afternoon. They sat on the hillside and watched us intently as we ate the donuts and washed and flapped our plates dry. As evening fell, the party music ended and the animals of the plains come out to drink and graze as the sun set over the Serengeti in a spectacular display of crimson.

Much later by lantern light, before bed, I heard laughter spilling from the back of the Bedford as everyone mingled around.

"See how much dirt there was on you face after all!!" I heard Sharon say triumphantly as she finished cleansing and toning Chris's face and showed him the cotton wool, black from African dust. A round of applause. How she made us laugh! Sharon, the corporate woman from Adelaide, having conquered her fears, had found her own unique place between the two worlds.

To awaken quite alone in a strange town
is one of the pleasantest sensations
in the world.

Dame Freya Stark: British Explorer, Author: *Baghdad Sketches*

Turkish Delight

For women, the best aphrodisiacs are words.
The G-spot is in the ears. He who looks for
it below there is wasting his time.

Isabel Allende, Chilean-American Author: *"Of Love and Shadows"*

As I ran headlong into the Liverpool airport, the clock struck 9.30 p.m. The "Direct Holidays" office staff had been waiting for me, and as they gave me one of those "girl where the hell have you been" looks, I was ushered frantically into the departure lounge. My international flight to Turkey was due to leave within the hour.

Only five hours earlier, frustrated and unable to find reasonably priced accommodation in Manchester, I had walked into a travel agency. "Direct Holidays" specialized in cutting out the middle-man and offered package holidays for Brits to exotic locations as Costa del Sol on the south coast of Spain; Portugal, the Caribbean, and the Turkish coast. Sun-drenched, all inclusive, white-washed 3-star hotels and package tours for the sun seeker were all there for the last minute tourist like me who wanted rock bottom prices.

"I have one ticket left for a one week package to Marmaris, Turkey on tonight's plane. There's a flight leaving at 10.30pm. I can get you on it luv but you'll have to move quickly. It leaves from Liverpool and that's one hour away by train."

Marmaris, Turkey? The thought of revisiting that beautiful town was deliciously inviting. I had little hesitation.

It was already 4.30 p.m. I did a mental time check. I was in downtown Manchester. Bus to Mark's apartment in the suburbs; pack; get back to the city; catch the 6.30 p.m. train to Liverpool; find my way out to the airport; International flight; I'd have to be there by 8.00pm. It was possible. I had my passport and my Visa card. I handed them over...

Of course, it hadn't been that simple. Falling into a seat in the airport waiting room I started to quietly chuckle with joy. Travelling Solo (TS) nudged me in the ribs grinning broadly and I laughed. If spontaneity was my mantra, then I sure had grabbed it by the collar. I stopped a sudden urge to jump up and dance in the crowded lounge. I was returning to Turkey!

· · · · · · · ● · · · · · · · ·

The phone rang unexpectedly and a shy, deep male voice asked me how I was.

"It's Aliihsan," he said. *"I was wondering you like me bring you cup coffee?"*

I had been working on my laptop all morning writing and was lost in my work. His kind offer was a pleasant surprise.

"That would be really lovely," I said. *"Thanks a lot".*

I put the phone down and smiled to myself. This would be interesting.

Aliihsan handed me the cup and sat on the opposite bed. I was suddenly aware of the intimacy of the situation. He seemed to be thinking about something.

"I wanted to talk to you" he smiled shyly.

We were in my large lovely attic hotel room at Club 55, a resort located on the hillside of Marmaris. The door to my private balcony was open and outside the sun was blazing down. It was a gorgeous blue sky autumn afternoon. Far away, yachts filled the upmarket marina and tourists strolled the boardwalks and bazaars. It was an incredibly beautiful time to be on the coast.

"Yesterday, Boris was very angry with me," he said. *"You went dancing last night, yes?"*

I nodded. The last twenty-four hours had indeed been quite fascinating. Within two hours of my arrival at the resort, my waiter Boris had invited me to go dancing later that night. He was attractive and confident.

"How old are you?" I had asked Boris in response to his invitation, noting his youthful looks.

"I am 23," he said. *"And you?"*

"Much older than you I'm afraid" I laughed.

"How old? 25?" He asked.

I could have kissed him right there. *"No, I'm 34"* I smiled.

He reeled in genuine disbelief. *"No, is not possible"*

"I think I heard that line on a television commercial" I laughed.

"What?"

I realized I had been too clever and spoken too fast. *"It doesn't matter, but thanks for the compliment"*

"You're welcome. 'So you want we go dancing? I meet you at 11.30 tonight yes?"

"Yes, alright" I had volunteered.

Later, at lunch that afternoon, while sitting at the pool bar, I had met Aliihsan, the drinks waiter. Gorgeous, dark, with beautiful clear olive skin, and a wide shy smile that brightened his entire face. He looked mature, gentle and much older than Boris, perhaps about 30.

"Are you going dancing tonight?" I had asked him, hoping he would be joining us as there was a group of travellers at the club and we had all agreed to meet later that night.

"Yes. Off course. You too? Will I see you tonight then?"

"Yes, I'm looking forward to it. See you at 11.30pm"

"Good OK. See you then," he said.

At dinner, the comedy of errors began.

"I will meet you at 11.30 tonight for dancing. Yes?" asked Boris as he brought me my meal.

"Yes, and I see Aliihsan is coming too"

"Who?"

"Aliihsan. Over there"

Boris looked confused and his smile fell. Before long, I could hear loud arguments coming from the kitchen, where the two guys were in obvious disagreement over the arrangements. The other dinner guests were looking towards the kitchen in surprise. I was conscious of the part I may have played in the mix-up. Boris appeared victorious from the kitchen to claim his prize and reconfirm our arrangements. Too late, I realized I had misinterpreted his intentions. We had a "date".

Amused by the situation I wondered how to handle it. Twenty years of dating and I was still not prepared for the delicate task of turning away this young man. After the first drink, when reaching for my hand, he declared his feelings for me. In amusement, I could only stifle a smile. I had no intention of becoming amorous with him but it appeared he was serious. I realized with surprise that I was embarrassed.

Trying to handle the situation delicately, I chose my words carefully.

"Boris, I am much older than you and I am not like you."

"You don't like me? he asked

"Yes I like you but I'm not like you"

"You don't like me?" he repeated.

"Yes Boris, I like you but not in that way"

"What way?"

I had to laugh. The conversation was making me giddy.

"I'm not interested in having a boyfriend right now."

"But I think you need sex," he said.

"Pardon?"

"You need sex. We all need sex. It is a natural thing, no?"

"No, I don't need sex right now, thanks"

"I think perhaps you have never have sex." It was a statement made as an observation. I was surprised.

"Boris, do you think that because I don't want to have sex with you that I have never had sex?"

This was followed by a pregnant pause. I let his comment pass, totally amused.

"I really like you," he said. *"You need boyfriend and I need girlfriend. Is simple, no? Why not?"*

"Boris, I don't need a boyfriend, and if I did, he would be 33 not 23."

"Why age is problem for you?"

I could foresee that the conversation would be going on for some time. I had to be brutally honest with him. When it was over I could see he was momentarily genuinely hurt and I knew he'd get over it pretty quickly, after all, he was waiting on many tables and the opportunities were many.

Back in my room, Aliihsan smiled, leaned close towards me and took my empty cup.

"Boris say to us you are his girlfriend".

He looked at me inquiringly. His tan was stunning next to his white shirt and I was momentarily distracted.

"Pardon?"

"Boris say to us you are his girlfriend".

I laughed. In the past, this would have annoyed me but not today.

"No, I'm not" I smiled, feeling suddenly quite warm and vulnerable.

"Then you want to meet me for drinks tonight?" His eyes looked steadily into mine and his eyebrows rose as he smiled.

"We talk, we walk, we see the moon. But we must meet away from here or Boris....." His words trailed away.

A clandestine meeting! I laughed, knowing I would go.

"How old are you?" I asked

"23" he replied.

But this time somehow, age really didn't matter........

• • • • • • • ● • • • • • • • •

"Cheap wine and a three-day growth, cheap wine and a three-day growth, come on........"

Cold Chisel's Australian rock classic from 1982 screamed from the CD player. My host, Tony, an award-winning Australian cinematographer was standing bent over in the yacht's saloon, mimicking Jimmy Barnes as he sang into his beer bottle. He was in another world, his eyes closed, passionately belting out the notes.

Some songs grip you at a certain age. The sound of them can bring back forgotten memories. I let myself fall back against the Beneteau's colourful cushions and laughed reminiscing about a young man who had sung that song to me many years earlier and stolen my heart as we made Cold Chisel's "East Album" our own. I felt pleasantly drunk. The warm evening rain had passed, the sky had cleared and moonlight was streaming through the open hatches.

I was on a fifty-five-foot yacht. Below deck the saloon was crowded. A private party for eight, beer, wine, tequila, salt, lemons and an international crowd. Steve whirled me to my feet and we joined Tony, dancing and singing, arms around each other. How had I got here? Who were these wonderful and happy people?"

I hadn't gone back to England as planned. Just the daunting thought of its cold grey skies and expensive accommodation sent my face sour. With my holiday package ending and one week to kill before my flight from Heathrow to JFK Airport in New York, I had contemplated my options:

(a) return to England and live like a starving tourist for seven days until my flight (b) return to my friend's home and plead insanely for floor space. Then a third option appeared.

"You must be Australian" I commented as I passed a very attractive blond backpacker standing on the boardwalk of the Marmaris marina.

"I haven't heard that accent in months. Where are you from?"

He had smiled warmly. *"Sure am mate. Sydney, but I'm working here now. Excuse my state. I've just got off a 36hr bus ride from Istanbul and I could do with a beer. I'm on my way to the bar. Like to join me?"*

It was as simple as that.

Entering the cool tiled bar, rattan fans whirling, the bartender greeted us warmly, exchanged welcoming laughter with Steve and taking his pack, he lead us to the balcony.

"Just put the beers on my tab, thanks" Steve had said.

I raised my eyebrows. Within the space of ten minutes, my life had once again changed. Stepping onto the balcony had suddenly opened a door into the upmarket, private and friendly world of international yachting. Over the next few days, I became fully immersed, met new people, and was welcomed with all the warmth of the rising sun.

The Marmaris marina was as full of money as I had remembered from our own bareboat yachting holiday years earlier when my friends and I had hired two Beneteau 39's and cruised the Turkish coast for two mind-blowing weeks. There were large imposing million dollar yachts, middle range 50 footers, sleek modern motor cruisers and expensive run-a-rounds baring colourful flags, expensive bottles of duty-free liquor and manned by crews relating stories of faraway lands, exotic ports, and adventures.

Steve was tanned, confident, attractive and unshaven with short blond hair. He had a typically masculine Australian laidback aura, which masked an intelligent, intense core. We both shared a love of writing, butterfly tattoos and he also spoke basic Spanish and enjoyed travelling. He laughed easily and was wonderfully articulate and knowledgeable on many levels. I was instantly drawn to this kindred soul. A qualified helicopter pilot, he had decided to take some time off to see the world. He had arrived in Marmaris months before at the beginning of the sailing season and had landed a crewing position on a 65ft commercial yacht with paying guests. His one week holiday in Istanbul now over, he had returned to Marmaris to get ready for the yacht's departure for the Seychelles, a journey which would take six weeks.

"You should hang around a few days," he said.

"There are lots of skippers in this town and lots of crew and interesting people. It's the end of the season and there are sure to be parties...."

"You're Australians, eh?"

It was a new face. Unshaven and much laid back, a man of indeterminable age, weathered from hours in the sunshine, took a seat at the next table and casually turned towards us holding his beer. He wore white loose sailing pants and an open-necked shirt. Bearded, with straight brown hair, he looked tired. Tony was the strong silent type, his own man. He had been hired to skipper a 55ft yacht from Thailand to Turkey and had taken a year off from his movie production company in Hong Kong to deliver the yacht. Having only recently arrived in Marmaris, his crew had departed and like me, had time on his hands while he awaited the yacht owner's arrival.....more beers.

The afternoon passed, stories were swapped and soon afternoon turned to evening. Tony had a colourful past. He had worked in current affairs and had travelled the war-torn corners of the world, filming painful and dangerous situations such as the 1989 student protests in China's Tiananmen Square. A veteran of his craft, his cinematography had earned him awards. Over the next few days, I slowly got to know both men better, sharing meals, meeting their friends and visiting bars and restaurants. And then one day, Tony had said magic words which were to change the course of my holiday.

"Well, why don't you move onto the yacht next week? You know your way around a yacht and I need a hand getting things ready. You can have your own cabin. All above-board. No need to go back to England"

Travelling solo (TS) can attract wanted and unwanted opportunities and a girl needs to know when to trust her intuition. After months of travelling alone, I knew a safe man when I met him so I allowed myself to flow with the opportunity the universe was providing. Inside, my heart burst into a spontaneous smile. In gratitude, the following week, I spent brilliant summer days scrubbing the hull, wet and dry sanding, varnishing and polishing brass all over the yacht in voluntary payment for my free board. Indeed, a small price to pay for my good fortune. The afternoons were spent writing, sunbathing, and visiting other yachts, shopping in the bazaars and drinking in the sunshine.

The party on board continued. As we danced and shot tequilas in the saloon, I felt overwhelmed with a crazy gaiety that I hadn't known in a while. We were eight travellers, pooled from five yachts, people from six different countries, speaking four different languages, travelling to vastly different destinations, possibly never to see each other again. Skippers crew members and ring-ins like me. Yet here, on a warm summer's night under a full moon in the Mediterranean we were partying together and celebrating what? I couldn't recall a reason. The end of the crewing season? A farewell? Or was it just to celebrate for the love of it? Or celebrating life? I think that was it.... cheap wine and three-day growths...

By midnight, convinced I was about to part company with my dinner, I climbed on deck for some fresh air. The tequila had hit me with a pleasant whirling sensation. Steve soon followed me. A marina at night is a special place of fairy lights, quiet water lapping next to sleeping hulls, the soft clink of halyards against masts, far away laughter and music on the breeze. And with the scenic view, my nausea disappeared.

Embracing warmly we inhaled the night marvelling at it all, whispering and then giggling like children, we climbed aboard Tony's dinghy and pushed off, drifting together on cushions, cuddling under blankets in the middle of the harbour. It was so peaceful and dark except for millions of stars above us and the twinkling lights of Marmaris on the shore.....

Little did we know that we would meet again in Indonesia in the months to come and that we would remain friends for the next few years, tied by those special memories.

Let's lay back, drink tequila, smoke cigarillos, and share some stories. TS

Pit Stop – A Mexican Train

*One should learn patience in a foreign
land, for this is the true measure of travel.
If one does not suffer some frustration, how
can one be sure one is really traveling?*

Gertrude Diamant, American Adventurer,
Author: *"The Days of Ofelia"*

"We're not leaving 'til 7.00pm!! Andrea's exasperated voice jolted me from my sleep and I slowly stretched. *"7 o'clock!!"*

The sun was still shining brightly on the Sierra Madre Oxidental mountains of northern Mexico, but our side of the valley was in shadow. I looked at my watch. It was 4.00p.m. The sun would set within the hour.

Five hours had already passed since our train, part of the Ferrocarriles Nacionales de Mexico, had slowly shunted into the dusty broken down village of Temoris. We were somewhere in the mountains en route to Creel, the small Mexican village where we were to spend the night. As twilight descended, our hopes of seeing Mexico's famous Copper Canyon faded. We would have to wait for the return journey down the valley. Our

Mexican camping trip was for the moment, experiencing a few problems and some people were getting riled.

I felt cold. The air conditioning had burst into action while I had been sleeping and goose bumps now covered my arms.

"Is it still hot outside?" I asked Andrea

"It's cool. The sun's going down. Better grab a jumper. We're over 1,000metres."

I smiled to myself. Andrea was Swiss and had learnt her English while travelling in Australia the year before. The term 'jumper' is a local Australian word for 'sweater' and her unconscious use of the word showed an honest mastery of the language. I envied her skills. I had spent the summer in Spain but I still couldn't swear with the conviction of a true Spaniard!

Through the cracked train windows, I could see the valley fall away below me to the right. Ramshackle stone buildings could be seen leaning precariously against each other far below us. Next to the train on the left, brown Mexican children dressed in rags chased each other and laughed, hiding amongst the carriages and shyly smiling at the foreigners.

In the sidings, three weathered Mexican men slumped in the shadows smoking, dressed in dirty bootleg jeans and cotton striped shirts. Their large white Gorachi cowboy hats were stained brown with sweat. They drew silently on cigarette stubs and grinned as they watched a colour party of poncho-clad locals play their violins further down the platform. Children were laughing and dancing around them in the late afternoon sunshine. My travelling companions sprawled on the dusty station platform playing cards, laughing and chatting. The hours had dragged on.

Two days earlier, eight miles up the line, the goods train from Los Moches to Creel had come off its tracks and five cars hauling ammonia were balanced precariously causing the Mexican authorities some concern. They had told us they needed three more hours to clear the tracks, then four. Now it looked like it would be eight. Ahh Mexico!

Pulling on my jumper, I jumped onto the platform and made my way up a small incline to a lopsided local diner where Jill was drawing contentedly on her cigarillo surveying the scene. An empty tin plate of tortillas and scrambled eggs lay in front of her.

She grinned. *"Only 3 more hours to kill!"*

I gave her a half-hearted smile and peeked into the dirt-floored kitchen behind her.

Two kindly Mexican women were busily making fresh tortillas, mixing flour and water and rolling the dough into small pancake shapes ready for frying. In the corner of the tiny room, there was an ancient wooden stove going full bore and bright red flames burst from the half open door. A hot buttered fry pan lay ready.

"Que quieres senorita? one asked me, not looking up from her work. (What do you want miss?)

"Tengo muy hambre señora. Me gustaria tortillas, huevos y chili por favor." I said, stating how hungry I was and ordering the same as Jill.

Their conversation filled the room and Jill exchanged thoughts and questions with the women through the open doorway. She was a thirty-two-year-old Californian, a very capable woman with a bohemian aura. She oozed that quiet confidence that solo travellers inherit from the road. I recognized it immediately and the TS woman in me admired her enormously for her peaceful resilience and ability to bend and adapt to whatever circumstances arose.

Jill spent half her year travelling and the other half working in a variety of jobs, eagerly looking forward to her next expedition. She had a courageous heart, a passion for travel and lived in the moment. Both in our thirties and single, I couldn't help but compare our lives. We shared a love for adventure, however, my journeys were often limited to six weeks whereon I would return to my comfortable career. I marvelled at how she handled the constant change, the instability of not knowing if a job was around the corner. When it came to money, I wanted enough of the stuff to live comfortably and to know I was financially secure to help me weather the cycles of life. I admired her ability to enjoy everything regardless of how the dice rolled.

"We're skirting down to the village to buy some tequila" Andrea said.

"Want to come?"

"Down there? We'd be lucky to get beer" I thought to myself peering down into the now dim valley. But, grasping the opportunity, I shook off my reluctance and with high spirits, we set off down the incline, three western women slipping and sliding on the scree slope whooping with delight as we descended into the twilight below. Arriving safely at the bottom in the main street, our options were few. Left or right?

"Donde compramos tequila senor?" I asked an old grizzled man watching us quietly from the shadows.

"A la izquireda directo" he intimated, pointing up the street to the left.

"Muchas gracias"!

Half an hour later back in the carriage, armed with a mean bottle of authentic Mexican tequila, lemons, salt, playing cards and sharing Jill's

American cigarillos, we drank, cheated at cards, laughed, puffed away and cared not, how long it would be, before our train's mournful whistle echoed through the canyons or when its pistons would lurch us forward into the now dark night. Inside our carriage, we were enjoying every moment.

Loving life is easy when you are abroad. Where no one knows you and you hold your life in your hands all alone, you are more master of yourself than at any other time.

Hannah Arendt: German Author: *"Rahel Varnhagen: The Life of a Jewess"*

December in Aspen

We have to learn to step back and know our thoughts and emotions are just thoughts and emotions.
They are just mental states.
We can change them if we choose

Vicki Mackenzie: British Buddhist nun.
Author: *"A Cave in the Snow"*

A silent hush had settled on the world as the snow muffled every sound. I stood ankle deep in powder between the fir trees and drank in the stillness. Christmas holidays had not yet begun and the mountain was empty of ski enthusiasts. Within a week, the crowds would start to build up, but for now, the mountains were mine. I had learnt to ski in Australia and was a keen enthusiast. Years ago I had had the good fortune to ski in Austria for one mesmerizingly beautiful week. Now, I was in the Colorado Rocky Mountains and simply couldn't believe my good fortune.

I took off my skis and immediately sank up to my knees. Joyful as a child, I allowed myself to fall backwards into the deep powder and looked up at the trees and the sky, recalling the words I had seen written in a photographic book at the Museum of Natural History in Denver:

"Before me peaceful;

Behind me peaceful;

Under me peaceful;

Over me peaceful;

All around me peaceful".

Navajo Indian

Behold this life and always love it.

It is very sacred, and you must treat it as such.

Sioux Indian

With all beings and all things,

We shall be as relatives.

Sioux Indian

I couldn't get those evoking words out of my mind. American Indians had for centuries roamed with the buffalo. Their spirit was here. Then in the 1500's the Spanish had introduced horses from Mexico and had changed forever the pace of life. While in Mexico, I had heard that centuries ago, the Indians near the border used to make long, tiring pilgrimages on foot to sacred sites, stopping and bowing and praying to their gods in gratitude. With the introduction of the horse, they had begun to ride to these sites. Now, some were seen to simply slow their pickup trucks and throw flowers on the sites before accelerating down the dusty roads on their way to shop at supermarkets. But their words still rang beautifully true and they stayed with me.

I stood and brushed off the snow but then fell over again, smiling. The trees and I were covered in it. Somewhere down the mountain, my travelling companions would be waiting for me, wondering where I was – but oh the beauty of solitude and powder snow in the mountains on a beautiful blue skied day!

*I haven't a clue as to how my
story will end. But that's
all right.
When you set out on a journey
and night covers the road,
you don't conclude the road
has vanished. And how else
could we discover the stars?*

Nancy Willard: American Author:
"Selected Poetry and Prose"

The Longest Ride

Leave behind the pressure to be perfect and begin the life-changing practice of simply being present, in the middle of the mess and the ordinariness of life.

Shauna Niequist: American Spirtual Author: *Present Over Perfect*

Grey skies. It was drizzling steadily as I climbed aboard and fell into a vacant Greyhound seat. The coach smelt of wet wool. The seats were half empty and long distance travellers glanced up at me, then out the windows in tired boredom, not that there was much to see. The windows were filthy grey, splashed with mud and whipped by the wind, rain and dirty snow, but it was warm inside. The doors swung closed and we pulled away onto Interstate 70, back into the weather.

I watched mesmerised as the enormous wipers laboured their way across the windscreen. Squeak bang, squeak bang. The snow sloshed and rain ran in rivulets horizontally off the windows. The soft outline of the Ski Mountains disappeared under fog and soon everyone in the coach was lulled to sleep as the afternoon wore on. We sped west through Colorado and away from the Rockies toward San Francisco.

I wondered, how many miles I had travelled on these coaches across America? The number seemed incomprehensible and the hours even more so. Down the East Coast from JFK in New York, through Washington DC to Norfolk, Virginia on the Chesapeake Bay. Then on through North and

South Carolina, the Blue Ridge Mountains and on to Georgia and Atlanta. I had coached it from Los Angeles south down Baja's arid Mexican deserts to Acapulco, Mexico City and back to LA, then northeast via Las Vegas to Denver and Boulder Colorado. Now here I was, leaving the Rocky Mountains behind as I headed across Utah to Salt Lake City, San Francisco and back to LA. Nearly US$800 in open-ended coach tickets, countless days and nights sitting, watching, reading, sleeping, but mostly listening and talking. In between towns, I stayed with friends or alone in inexpensive hotels.

The truth is that I had discovered the unparalleled joy of travelling solo. Give me an economical way to travel, meet local people and the ability to go as the wind does and I'm satisfied and happy. Greyhound was my ideal way to explore America, as it required little more than a tolerance for sitting still for long periods and an interest in characters that would ordinarily never cross my path. Somewhere between New York and Los Angeles, I was initiated and warmly accepted into the world of the long distance coach traveller, to locals with time on their hands and little money in their wallets. We exchanged stories, food, laughter, and opinions and shared the dreaded rear washroom that emitted the foul smell of chemical pollutants and undigested junk food. Our confined world drew us together.

My companions were unforgettable people, open talkative travellers of black, white, Hispanic, and Southeast Asian lineage. A hodgepodge of drifters, grandparents, Indians, ex-cons, runaway youths, religious zealots, dreamers, and battlers. People, who voluntarily swapped information, chatted with passing strangers who chanced to sit next to them through a long afternoon or shared night. People going places to find work, to visit friends, to have holidays, to see children. People just moving on. I had only two more days of coach travel before I would finally arrive back in LA. My mind drifted, remembering the faces I had met over the last 3 months. It had all started in Manhattan.

• • • • • • • • ● • • • • • • • • •

*"**O.K. LISTEN UP** back there people. This is the Greyhound coach to WASHINGTON DC and I am your driver. This coach is equipped for your convenience with a washroom at the rear. There is to be **NO smoking***

or consumption of alcoholic beverages OF ANY KIND on the coach ye hear?
That includes the washroom! No smoking! Private music systems may be played
with the use of headsets but man, if I can hear it - **IT'S TOO LOUD! NOW**
PEOPLE - ENJOY THE RIDE!

I had stopped a compulsion to laugh and salute and turned and looked at the other passengers. They were all grinning. We had just left Manhattan's Port Authority Terminal on 42nd Street. Our driver was a big mama of a woman, an African-American with loads of attitude, false two-inch fingernails with glitter studs and long blond straight plaited hair, which looked strangely out of place next to her black skin. She was very overweight and the seams of her grey uniform pantsuit were strained to the limit. I noticed white socks. She grunted and pushed the microphone away from her as she grabbed the wheel with both hands and swung the coach toward the George Washington Bridge, over the Hudson River, and toward the New Jersey State line.

• • • • • • • ● • • • • • • • •

The Rockies were slowly diminishing in size. Through the bleak grey windows, I could see flatter terrain and a town in the distance, which might be Grand Junction. It had stopped raining. Everyone was asleep and I stretched out further on my double seat, happy to be alone, remembering and reminiscing.

• • • • • • • ● • • • • • • • •

A young attractive guy was sitting alone in the Greyhound terminal in Washington. He was fair, wore blue jeans and a white T-shirt. I imagined him to be about twenty-five, possibly a carefree backpacker touring the world. When we finally climbed aboard the coach to Norfolk, Virginia he sat next to me. I was wrong.

It was mid-October and Fall had well and truly arrived in all its autumn glory. The highway was lined with full-grown maples and spruce, enormous trees resplendent in yellows, reds, purples, and oranges creating a scenic view. Mile after mile of four-lane asphalt was lined with shimmering leaves,

179

all the colours of the rainbow, which danced and played in the sunshine as our coach raced toward the Chesapeake Bay and the Atlantic Ocean.

Jeff had been working in Miami and was returning home to Virginia. A keen surfer and sun lover, he had moved around trying out a variety of jobs that were mostly associated with outdoor sports. He was living so far from home and he really missed his family and friends. His elderly mother needed help with the house and he was heading back to his home in Norfolk for a few months to help and spend time with his mum leading up to Christmas. He came from a big family and we swapped stories of the festive season, the heat of an Australian Christmas with its gourmet seafood, cold ham, salads and champagne versus the snow and warmth of Virginia's traditional hot turkey dinner, puddings, and open fires. By the time we arrived at the Chesapeake Bay, Jeff had invited me to spend Christmas with his family.

"But you hardly know me!" I had exclaimed.

"Do you often invite strange women to your mother's house for Christmas dinner?"

"No, but hey, why not? You'll be alone in America and we have a big, family Christmas. It would be fun. You can see how Americans celebrate" he had answered.

"Here's my address. Keep in touch and let me know if you'd like to come OK? You'd be very welcome."

I left him standing on the road in Norfolk, warmed by his open hospitality, wondering if I *would* see him again. Christmas still seemed a lifetime away.

• • • • • • • • ● • • • • • • • • •

My coach had left Colorado and was heading west into Utah, which is a beautiful state. The Colorado Mountains flatten out into a dry and rugged desert hewn by wind and water. Thousands of years of erosion have left gigantic carved mesas, buttes and plateaus throughout the region; they are like silent sentinels guarding the red landscape. Enormous boulders, the size of buildings, overshadow hardy native desert plants. Even through the gloomy windows, I could see the colours so reminiscent of the Australian outback. Reds, oranges, and copper glowed in the fading evening light.

An attractive young black woman was in conversation with the driver about Australia. Curious, I made my way to the front of the coach, introduced myself and was soon engrossed in a fascinating account of her life.

"Chloe" wasn't very American at all. Her father was a black American preacher, who had married a French woman and migrated to France. She had been brought up in Paris under the strict guidance of her pious parents. Jeans, makeup, adornments of any type were banned from the household and boyfriends had to pass the strictest questioning by her father. Consequently, boyfriends never lasted very long.

When her parents died during her teens, she was sent to live with her godparents who shared similar values and upbringing. When both godparents died in a car crash she was sent to live in a nunnery. It had been the wish of her father that she should devote her life to serving the poor. Miserable and unhappy and realising her total naiveté about the world, she packed her bags and secretly fled France. Now here she was, on a Greyhound heading to the Canadian border with her entire possessions packed into six cardboard boxes and four canvas bags. With these possessions, she hoped to begin a new life. She had no friends in America and knew nothing of Canada but felt drawn to live amongst French-speaking people. She travelled with no maps or guidebooks and felt no concern at the prospect of arriving in Vancouver at 1.30 a.m. with all her luggage and no pre-booked accommodation. I, on the other hand, said a silent prayer for her safety and tried to determine if her enthusiastic plans bubbled from sheer naiveté or unlimited courage.

"You know, it's so strange here in America," she said, consciously lowering her voice to a whisper.

"I look like a black American and people think I am, but I have nothing

181

in common with these people. I'm French. I hate American food man and our customs are so different. You know when I first got here and I met people, I would kiss them on both cheeks like we all do in France. Well, this black chick she just jumped two feet clear away from me and shouted. "What the hell are you doing girl? You a lesbian or something?!"

I started to laugh despite myself. Chloe was so animated and passionate in her storytelling that I was totally drawn into her life and found myself sympathizing, totally amused at the situations she had encountered.

"I have to watch everything I do and say, even with the blacks," she said. *"And you know what? In all my years in France I never felt self-conscious about my colour, yet in America man, I am always conscious of it. I don't understand why it's an issue in this country. But there are lots of good things too. I can dress up and make myself look pretty good if I want and no one minds. Hell, if my father could see me wearing these jeans and these here sneakers...."* She raised her eyebrows. *"Man this is a new me!"*

I couldn't help smiling. Chloe was an attractive woman, with beautiful clear black skin, a high forehead and braided hair extensions. She wore jewellery and makeup and was obviously enjoying her newfound freedom that had been denied her for so many years.

"What are you going to do in Canada?" I asked, curious to know about her plans.

"Well, I tell you what". Her voice was barely audible now and she leant toward me. Curious, I watched her face as she spoke.

"I want to find me a husband but I'll tell you something. It's hard you know 'cause after all these years, what with my strict father and all, I've never had no boyfriend and I'm still a virgin! Now, what kind of man is going to want me? Hell, I'm twenty-seven years old!" She seemed momentarily self-conscious by her confession.

"So I was thinking that perhaps I should let that little piece of information just pass on by and maybe he'll never know" she giggled. *"I was thinking,*

like, I might go to a really nice hotel in Vancouver you know, and do myself up real nice. Then I'll go down to the bar and sit there all done up with my hair an' all and I'll order one of those big glasses of Perrier with a slice of lime you know. I've seen that in the movies. So I'll sit there and I'm sure I'll meet a man that way. I mean I know I'm not beautiful but I can make myself look pretty good. So what do you think?"

I was spellbound and uncharacteristically speechless for a moment.

"Well, I'm sure you'll meet a man that way Chloe but I'm not sure that he will be the marrying type" I smiled kindly.

"What do you really enjoy doing?"

She looked surprised. *"Well, I like the theatre and reading literature… stuff like that."*

"Well, maybe you could find people who also like doing that type of thing. If you do what YOU really want to do, chances are you'll find someone with very similar interests and he will be far more the marrying type because you'll have more in common…." I heard myself talking. Even though logical and sensible, it hadn't worked for me.

The huddled silhouettes of Utah's western country towns raced by. With the approaching evening, oases of bright town lights flashed by and then disappeared. In the darkness, a gigantic rock monoliths rose, silhouetted against the rising moon. A young black man was snoring, curled up warmly in his seat. While I watched him, faces and entertaining conversations came back to me.

• • • • • • • • ● • • • • • • • • •

The first black man that I ever spoke to had been on a Greyhound coach, a night trip in Georgia, en route to Athens that Fall. His name was Jimmy. He was a solid man, about thirty-five years of age with short-cropped black hair and a pleasant face. For safety, I preferred to sit near the front of the coach near the driver, especially when travelling alone at night and I had been lucky to book the front seat. As Jimmy fell into the seat next to me he introduced himself.

"You travelling alone girl?" he asked in amazement.

"Mind if I sit here? I won't mind you no trouble..."

It was a warm night in Georgia. The sky was full of stars and the coach's windscreen was sparklingly clear. We had an uninterrupted view of the highway and a talkative driver to keep us company. Jimmy was divorced. His two children were with his wife. He was working for a manufacturing company that had offered him a transfer to Australia but he was unsure about how he would be treated as a black American.

"The Aborigines are black right?" He had asked.

"I thought so. So how do you think I'd get along down there? I don't want no trouble you know..."

He was interested in racism and the history of the Aboriginal people. He spoke intelligently about the problems of the American South, its informal separatism and underlying racism which was still evident despite the illegalities of segregation. I told him about the Aborigines and he told me about the Martin Luther King museum in Atlanta. He spoke with no animosity toward the whites, only a quiet sadness when referring to the past and when telling me about his marriage.

I told him of my interest in experiencing real southern food such as grits, black-eyed peas, fried chicken, jambalaya, fried green tomatoes, beef jerky, sweet potato pie, crayfish pie, fillet gumbo. As I rattled off the names of all those dishes Jimmy started to laugh.

"Hey hol' on girl. How you know all them foods ....you from Australia an all.?"

I told him how I had seen and heard them in American movies and songs. He was amazed.

"Hell, all I know about yaw food is them shrimps on the bar-b-que. What's that's guy's name. Paul Hogan? Cro...o...dile Dun...dee. Hell, that was a movie. You really got crocks down there? Hell, I'd luv ta see one o them kangaroos too but the food...nope don't rightly know much 'bout that." He chuckled to himself.

"You want ta eat re...al southern food, you need ta know where ta go en Athens," he said. *"You got a bi...ro? I can tell you some places...safe like...where the blacks eat real food."*

And that was how I got to know Jimmy. I told him I wanted to go to a black Sunday Baptist church service and hear the singing I had seen and heard in so many movies. He told me about the Ebenezer Baptist Church in Athens, which was in a safe district where I would be welcomed as a white person.

When we arrived in Athens, he stood and smiled and shook my hand warmly with genuine affection and then disappeared quickly into the night before I had the chance to introduce him to my white southern friends. I'm not sure if they would have approved anyway.

• • • • • • • • ● • • • • • • • • •

My coach neared Salt Lake City, where I bid Chloe farewell. The city's sprawling immensity glowed brightly in the darkness as we approached. Night had fallen and alighting for a half-hour layover I felt cool under the now clear star-studded winter sky. The Greyhound terminal was overflowing with travellers and their possessions. Tired people could be seen resting on dirty floors surrounded by luggage while they killed hours waiting for connections. Well-dressed travellers stood impatiently, eagle eyes anxiously guarding their luggage against wondering thieves. A young woman with a lip and nose stud, who looked like she'd been around the block a few times, was passionately tongue kissing her boyfriend goodbye. A middle-aged Vietnam vet wondered aimlessly through the terminal, spitting profanities at the world, oblivious to everyone's stares. They were a mass of strangers heading west toward the Pacific, beautiful San Francisco and every small town in between. No doubt, the coach would be full for the next leg and I would hear yet another story. I smiled in anticipation as I sat, wondering which of the surrounding faces it would be. I didn't have long to wait.

"Rifle" was built like his name, wore blue jeans, plaid shirt, and a jumper and looked rough like an underfed truckle. I could see his angular profile in the darkness next to me as we pulled onto the interstate and headed west. I asked him where he was going.

"Oh only about 200 miles up the road" he answered with a tired voice. *"Won't be too long".*

He smelt of old booze. Rifle was middle aged. His wife had died of cancer at age forty, leaving him with a three-year-old beautiful blond daughter and a five-month-old son. He was a diesel mechanic, who was returning home to see his children who were being cared for by their grandparents in a small town north of 'Frisco. His job took him all over Utah for weeks at a time. He needed the work and was finding it tough to look after the kids.

"Thank God for grandparents" he sighed.

"Don't know what I'd do without 'em"

Taking a photo from his wallet, he turned on the overhead light in the now-darkened coach and with pride showed me a photo of his family. His wife had been an attractive woman. His kids were cute. They had been reasonably well off and had gone snow skiing and hiking in the holidays. His voice was soft as he spoke of his wife recalling things they had done together. His wife had had a small life insurance policy but after she died he was forced to move into a trailer with his kids. He had somehow managed to buy them a VCR and had installed cable TV. He was a lonely soul, sad, a battler.

He knew the entire Salt Lake area and pointed out landmarks to me in the gloom as we raced along. He talked and talked, his voice slowly drifting off as his eyes glazed over. Then he fell asleep and I looked out into the night, thanking God for my good fortune in life and silently wishing more for him. At 2.00 a.m. we pulled into a tiny town on the outskirts of nowhere.

"Hey look after yourself. Will you call me from Australia when you get back? No? Well, thanks for being honest. Can't blame you but thanks for the chat"

And without another word he was gone. I felt a little sad, curled up and dozed, dreaming of my family and the bright Australian summer.

Small western towns came and went throughout the night. In an all-night diner north or Frisco at 4:00 a.m., I fell into conversation with a country and western fiddle player from Nashville. I stifled a sleepy yawn, noting his typical country and western Stetson, bootleg jeans and guitar carved bronze belt buckle. It struck me as delightful to see the incarnation of American television stereotypes come to life as I travelled around the country. After months of playing in a band, he was headed home to Frisco for a break to write some new songs. He was quiet and seemed a gentle soul who was not into glamour or false pretences - well not at that hour of the morning anyway. We both were travel-worn, crumpled and in need of hot showers and comfortable beds. The diner food was inedible, greasy and stale. As we drank our steaming coffee, he looked sadly at the stuffed majestic white polar bear standing at least 2.5m tall which guarded the door to the diner.

"Such a beautiful animal isn't it? Now why did someone have to go and kill something as beautiful as that?"

I agreed. Such were our whimsical reflections of life at 4:00 a.m.

• • • • • • • ● • • • • • • • •

"Don't you touch that bag, lady. I mean it. No one touches these bags unless I inspect their tickets. I mean it, lady. Leave that bag! Hey you! If you take that bag lady, you're stealing. Lady! Lady! Hey you, bitch, come back here!!!!"

A tall black woman with a seven-year-old son, threw her baggage claim ticket at the baggage hand, grabbed her bag and raced into the terminal to catch her connecting coach, her son streaming behind her like a sea anchor. The colourful language brought a gasp from us all as we watched. It had taken far too long to unpack the luggage hole and everyone was impatient.

"Let her go you jerk, she showed you the ticket"

"Hey, how about our bags man? Hurry the hell up"

"Get off her case you asshole and let her go!"

The woman had the crowd on her side as she ran and was already inside the terminal, the luggage man in hot pursuit. The crowd looked at each other, started to chuckle and without another moment's hesitation, all lunged for their bags before he could return. Within a minute, all that was left was an empty trolley.

I met the woman racing out of the washroom and grinned.

"You had the crowd on your side" I laughed.

"That arsehole got the sack man - on the spot! His boss heard him call me a bitch. What a nerve."

We laughed and I wished the courageous lady well. Coach terminals with all their travellers were never boring! It was morning and San Francisco was still a few hours away. I boarded my connecting coach and watched the scenery change to rolling green hills as we neared California. Soon there would be palm trees. I thought of Mexico.

On an almost nonstop forty-eight hour coach trip from tropical Mexico City north to Tijuana, on an almost empty coach, I had chanced to meet Monse. She was Mexican, twenty-four, highly strung, excitable and spoke quickly in Spanish. This attractive young woman with a dark, olive complexion and manicured nails was well-groomed with a love for lots of makeup and nice clothes. She was travelling only a short distance of about 100 miles to meet her boyfriend for whom she had bought an American baseball cap, which she proudly showed me. She had saved hard and had bought it with her wages. Monse worked as a secretary and as the oldest, had supported her family of five brothers and one sister ever since their parents died. They all lived at home in a two-bedroom house in a tiny Mexican village.

Did I like the cap? Did I really? Did I think her boyfriend would like it? Where was I going and why was I traveling alone? Wasn't I scared? Why wasn't I married? Did I have a boyfriend? Why didn't I wear make-up? Did I think her clothes were pretty? Did I really? How long did it take to get to Australia and would I like to have her address?

As the north Mexican desert sun beat down relentlessly through the coach windows, I watched the cacti prickle in the heat. These people so loved to talk. She wanted to be like the Americans. When she got off the coach, she waved to me, smiling by the side of the road in the dusty haze of an outback town. Her baseball cap was safely wrapped up in her pretty basket. I wondered why her makeup didn't melt in the heat.

By the time we reached Tijuana, I was very hungry. I had spent long hours travelling from Mexico City with short layovers in dusty towns, drinking warm coke and limp tortillas. The closer we came to the border, the more crowded the coach had become. Then in Tijuana, a 65-year-old Filipino grandmother got on. Rose, like me, was headed back to Los Angeles. Clucking, shoving and bundling her shy husband in front of her, she had collapsed into the seat next to mine. Her lap disappeared under bags of food, cold drinks and magazines. She had come prepared and without any hesitation, Rosie began to eat.

Conscious of how loud my stomach was rumbling, I immediately turned away towards the window but the loving soul that she was, within seconds, was tugging on my arm, offering me some of her picnic. It was only then that I realised that Rose, the shy and gentle Filipino woman was the most vivacious, uplifting and happy woman I had met in all my travels. Oh, how she laughed, recalling her first year in the USA, her fears and timidity to even leave her house.

"And look at me now!" she exclaimed.

"I go everywhere, ask everyone questions, and seek answers. I have travelled all over the USA alone staying with my friends and family. Oh, now I have friends everywhere, EVERYWHERE! My sons are all grown men, engineers, and teachers".

She continued to chuckle and eat from her plastic bag of Triscuits, which sprung a leak and covered the seat in cracker shreds. Rose just clucked and laughed and continued unabashedly telling me about her family, all the opportunities open to them now in the US and how wonderful it all was.

"Because in the United States you can do anything," she said, unscrewing a little bottle of ginger ale and carefully pouring it into two plastic cups, one for each of us.

"Always make sure you ask questions and travel with lots of food" she confided, holding onto my arm as she leaned toward me, winked and smiled.

By the time we pulled into the LA coach terminal, her picnic bag was empty. We hugged farewell and I watched her drag her husband toward the inquiry counter.

· · · · · · ● ● ● ● ● ● ● ● · · ·

Awaking from my daydream, the skyline of San Francisco greeted me. Finally, I had arrived. I was to spend a few days visiting Ann, an American friend that I had made by chance at a bed and breakfast hotel in London. She like so many hospitable Americans had invited me to her home. It was an opportunity not to be missed. One week of sightseeing in that glorious city, late night talks, lots of seafood and wine and I was back in the Greyhound terminal for the last leg of my journey south to LA from where I would fly back to Australia. As I climbed the steps of the coach and found my seat for the last time, I felt slightly forlorn.

Even in winter, California is clean, big and beautiful. As I neared LA I marvelled at its great southern freeway linking 'Frisco for hundreds of miles south of the Mexican border. The Palm trees stood erect in the crisp, cold sunshine, and expansive views of the Atlantic Ocean stretched before me, its cold breakers, crashing onto now deserted beaches. It had been an immense solo journey and I was ending it as I had begun, alone, with a double window seat, smiling to myself.

Somewhere out there, across the hundreds of thousands of miles that is America, people I had met would be rugged up, getting ready for Christmas. Some like Jeff, Rose and Monse would be with their families, laughing and exchanging gifts, surrounded by love and the warmth of the season. Others like Jimmy, Rifle and Chloe would possibly be very much alone, travelling different paths to a different rhythm. They were only three of America's thousands of isolated individuals, many from broken families, many with sad hearts. All were the type of people who would ordinarily never have crossed my path, but knowing them, for even a short while had made my appreciation of life so much richer.

In three days, I would be boarding a Qantas flight back to the Australian summer, to a warm Christmas Eve full of friends, family, and laughter from people I longed to tenderly embrace with eyes now wide open. I had shamelessly yearned to open a door to a different standard of life and adventure and had found in me, a renewed respect, admiration and gentleness for us all. It was time to go home.

An Invitation

If you have stepped through your comfort zone to a new level of courage and fun and felt the power of TS in your life, share it with us on Facebook **@tsbreakthroughs**.

I'd love to hear from you.

Juliette

Epilogue

*We were made to be awesome and beautiful
and brilliant. You know that! Own it! TS*

We are much bigger on the inside than we think. Whatever you call her, Travelling Solo, your True Self, TS is Divine, funny, challenging and always present. She is the hero in you that you wish to be.

We are all travelling solo in life but we are never alone, for TS is inside us all, whispering in our ears and stirring our hearts.

Although we don't often expect it, incredible kindness, help and generosity do await us if we embrace others with an open heart. TS has thrown me into countless unexpected, delightful and sometimes dangerous situations that tested my humour and my resolve but the more I surrendered to the opportunities around me, the more help and guidance I received. There is a wonderful feeling of vulnerability, excitement and strength in surrendering to the unknown.

We are all connected on this journey. We can transcend the mundane and make our daily lives into the amazing adventures that we desire.

Look for the opportunities in each day, stay flexible, follow the gentle nudges of your spirit, listen to each other, speak your truth and step courageously and deliberately into the unknown with a smile in your heart.

Juliette

About Juliette

Juliette was born in Kandy Sri Lanka, grew up in Adelaide and lives in Sydney Australia. She is a senior Learning and Development Business Consultant, Executive Coach and Facilitator, helping managers to step up to a bigger vision of all that is possible. As an adventure traveller she has backpacked, trekked, sailed, trucked, dived, skied and flown to over 50 countries. Juliette and her husband Guy have two children, Jordon and Lauren. They live on Scotland Island in Pittwater on Sydney's northern beaches.

Also by Juliette Robertson

Journeys: A Robertson / Marshall Anthology

A family anthology that captures the romance, struggle, beauty and personal memories of two large British Burgher Railway families growing up in Sri Lanka in the 1900's. © 2002

Water Access Only: Tales and Images from Pittwater

An anthology of funny and poignant short stories, poems, beautiful photography and artwork from residents of Scotland Island and the Western Foreshores of Pittwater, that capture the essence of what it's like to live an 'offshore' lifestyle, where the only way to get home is by boat. ©2006